SATIRIST.

AY, SEPTEMBER 6, 1845   Vol. 8.

R BASTILE.

THE COMMISSION OF INQUIRY DISCUSSING THE SUBJECT OVER
A GOOD DINNER.

Graham if he had heard " that the paupers of a Union in Hampshire were employed
, in extracting marrow from them, and in gnawing off the meat from the extremities.
) which has taken place into this truly shocking affair, that the paupers are employed in
animals, and " occasionally" some from churchyards.
we have it in the words of the paupers themselves that they are ' ready to fight over the
, and hides it till he gets an opportunity of gnawing it.'"—DISPATCH.

THE SCANDAL OF
THE ANDOVER WORKHOUSE

The Scandal of the Andover Workhouse

IAN ANSTRUTHER

GEOFFREY BLES

THE SCANDAL OF THE ANDOVER WORKHOUSE
is published by Geoffrey Bles
59 Brompton Road, London SW3 1DS

ISBN: 0 7138 0590 0

© Ian Anstruther, 1973

Printed in Great Britain by
The Anchor Press Ltd and bound by
Wm. Brendon & Son Ltd, both of Tiptree, Essex

FOR SUSAN

Acknowledgements

In a book of this sort which has to supply a wide general background for a detailed local event, an author is helped by two quite different groups of experts. There are those who guard the national archives, whose mastery of their contents permits the historian to consult documents which, otherwise, he would never find; and those who painstakingly preserve local records, without whose co-operation the student of local history could discover nothing. In the ordinary way they never meet although their work has equal importance. It is my privilege, in this book, to express my gratitude to both.

I thank formally the Comptroller of H.M. Stationery Office for permission to quote Crown Copyright material in the Public Record Office; the Hampshire County Archivist for authority to quote from the papers of the Andover Poor Law Union; His Grace the Duke of Portland and the University of Nottingham for sanction to quote from the Bentinck papers; the Librarian of University College, London, for leave to quote from the Chadwick papers; The Rector of Weyhill for licence to quote from the Poor-Rate Books of that parish; the Vicar of Amport for liberty to quote from the Amport Vestry Minutes.

I am grateful to the following for information about the quality and energy content of bread in the early 19th century: the Keeper of the Museum of English Rural Life at the University of Reading; Mr. E. N. Greer, O.B.E., B.Sc., A.R.I.C., Deputy Director of the Flour Milling and Baking Research Association; Mr. M. St. A. Hartley, Director of W. Prewett Ltd.; Mr. J. Luke, Commercial Manager of Joseph Rank Ltd.

My thanks are due to the undermentioned for information concerning Colonel a'Court: Mrs. M. A. Welch, Keeper of

Manuscripts at the Library of the University of Nottingham; Dr. John Rosselli, Reader in History at the University of Sussex; Mr. D. W. King, Librarian at the Ministry of Defence.

For kind permission to reproduce their illustrations in this book I would like to thank the following: Illustrations 1 and 2, F. Holmes Esq; 3, Charles Green Esq; 4 and 5, the Comptroller of H.M. Stationery Office; 6, Miss J. E. Lee; 7, the Trustees of the National Portrait Gallery; 8, John Elliot Esq; 9, Lord Heytesbury; 10, Mrs. W. B. Hawley; 11 and 12, *The Times*. The endpapers are from a cartoon reproduced by permission of the Trustees of the British Museum.

I thank personally my secretary, Barbara Copeland, for typing this MS many times, and Dr. and Mrs. Eldon Stowell, Miss Aldred and Richard Ollard for reading it and making suggestions and corrections. I am truly grateful to George Brickell, Secretary of the Andover Local Archives Committee, for placing his encyclopaedic knowledge at my disposal on many, many occasions. I thank Michael Franklin, Officer in Charge at Ashridge and Melville Child of Appleshaw. I thank last, although he comes first, Kenneth Timings, Principal Assistant Keeper at the Public Record Office. He suggested that I write this book. I have enjoyed doing it. I shall always be grateful to him.

I. A.

Contents

Illustrations

xi

Preface

THE 19TH CENTURY Workhouse System which came into being in 1834 and which, in effect, nationalised the poor, was the first major social reform to follow the great **Reform Act**. Brought about by changing times—industrialisation, unemployment and a rapid increase in the population—it established a pattern of social relief which lasted for more than one hundred years. Had it worked the way it was planned as a self-operating test of need, providing humane care for the indigent and deterring the idle from sponging off the rates, it might have proved a benefit to all. In the event, it punished the poor for even demanding the right to eat, and, by many cruel economies, cutting the cost of relief to the bone, achieved substantial savings in the rates to the benefit only of those who grudgingly paid them.

No one, however, can study its history or read the findings of the Royal Commission which advised the Government to adopt the System without being struck by the good intentions, the kindly approach and crusading hopes of those who took such pains to devise it. A new measure for a new age, based on the latest political theories that the best laws operate themselves to the greatest good of the greatest number, it was passionately felt by all its supporters to signal the approach of a better era. In the end, events betrayed them. Uncontrollable economic forces, doctrinaire administration, and the greed and cruelty of petty officials, all combined to prove them wrong. When they saw the System's defects—its heartless lack of flexibility, its total failure to protect minorities—it had been in force for more than a decade. Understanding came too late; and another chance to realise their vision never, unhappily, returned.

In the study that follows on the Poor Law Commission and the Union Workhouse at Andover in Hampshire, it is necessary

xiii

to mention certain omissions. Nothing has been said of the law of settlement, nor of the difficult question of bastardy. Both these were very important but do not happen to come into the story. The detailed history of the Poor Law is vast. The background here has been kept to the absolute minimum. It is also important to make the point that much that is said about Andover and Hampshire did not apply to places in the north and especially to London, Birmingham and Manchester. Urban problems were quite different and could not be treated with the same simplicity although for a time this was not accepted. But much of what has been said about Hampshire and much of the treatment that the poor received there had exact parallels throughout the south. The balloon happened to go up at Andover, not because conditions were worse but only because of special circumstances. It is these particular local events that make the story so interesting.

Lastly, nothing has been said at all about changing 19th-century attitudes, especially those of the established church, towards the poor and charity and poverty. Had the evolving pattern of industry not created a different world, and had the public been less alarmed by the obvious popular discontent, the Workhouse System might not have been adopted. The frightening increase in the numbers of the poor, also the marked decline in their respect, made a defensive system imperative.

Thus the social stratas developed which became such a feature of Victorian society. To attempt to escape them became a sin, condemned alike by the public and the church. Over and over and over again, the poor were advised to accept their lot, and not to stain their souls by rebellion. This was noticeably so at Andover. To point it out would have been unnecessary. The documents record the shameful tale themselves.

PART ONE

The Workhouse

'The workhouse should be a place of hardship, of coarse fare, of degradation and humility; it should be administered with strictness—with severity; it should be as repulsive as is consistent with humanity . . .'

The Revd. H. H. Milman to Edwin Chadwick, 1832.

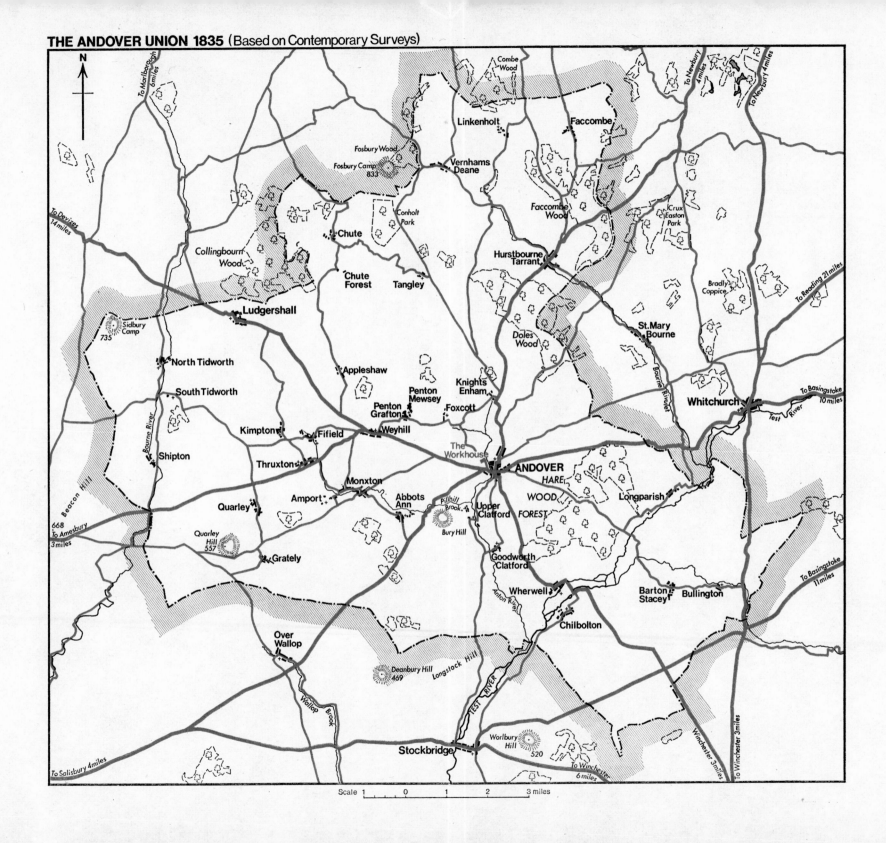

THE ANDOVER UNION 1835 (Based on Contemporary Surveys)

N

To Marlborough 6 miles

To Devizes 14 miles

Combe Wood

Linkenholt

Faccombe

Fosbury Wood

Fosbury Camp 833

Vernhams Deane

Conholt Park

Faccombe Wood

Crux Easton Park

Chute

Hurstbourne Tarrant

To Newbury 4 miles

To Newbury 4 miles

Collingbourn Wood

Chute Forest

Tangley

Bradly Coppice

To Reading 21 miles

Ludgershall

Sidbury Camp 735

Doles Wood

St. Mary Bourne

North Tidworth

Appleshaw

Knights Enham

South Tidworth

Penton Mewsey

Foxcott

Bourne River

Whitchurch

To Basingstoke 10 miles

Penton Grafton

Test River

Kimpton

Fifield

Weyhill

The Workhouse

Shipton

Thruxton

ANDOVER

HARE

Longparish

Beacon Hill

Monxton

Abbots Ann

Pillhill Brook

WOOD

Quarley

Amport

Bury Hill

Upper Clatford

FOREST

668

To Amesbury 3 miles

Quarley Hill 557

Grately

Goodworth Clatford

Barton Stacey

Bullington

To Basingstoke 11 miles

Wherwell

Anton River

Chilbolton

Over Wallop

Deanbury Hill 469

Longstock Hill

TEST RIVER

To Winchester 3 miles

Wallop Brook

Worlbury Hill 520

To Salisbury 4 miles

Stockbridge

To Winchester 6 miles

Winchester 3 miles

Scale 1   0   1   2   3 miles

Chapter 1

WHEN WILLIAM IV succeeded to the throne at the start of the third decade of the 19th century, a multitude of urgent and dangerous problems, most of them new and all of them baffling, lay in threatening confusion before his Government.

Superficially, the origin of each was different. Depression had hit the industrial north and thousands were homeless and out of work; terrible storms had destroyed the crops and everywhere the poor were hungry and in rags; tens of thousands, literally, had died when cholera, India's dreaded scourge, had ravaged the country with inexorable speed; everywhere riot, arson and sabotage threatened the nation with civil war as popular clamour for political reform, dangerously muted since the French Revolution, erupted at last with frightening, incalculable force.

Yet, manifold though these crises were, all were alike in their size and complexity; if each required a different remedy, all were bedevilled by a common cause. For during the previous thirty years since the first census of 1801 the population had increased by two thirds and now stood at almost fifteen millions. No one knew the reason for this—nobody, indeed, is sure of it today—but whatever it was it created extra difficulties. Whichever way the Government looked and whichever subject they began to tackle, unmanageable numbers of people seemed to be involved.

There was, for example, the problem of caring for the poor. Due to a series of complicated factors which were not then understood, their numbers had mounted to such an army that even to feed them had almost become impossible. The cost alone was astronomical, more than seven million pounds per year; and since, because of an economic spiral, the more it mounted every year the more it created unemployment, it

17

presented the poor as well as the rich with a puzzle that seemed insoluble.

The paupers, however, naturally enough were not concerned with the trials of the ratepayers. Towards the end of 1830, hungry, homeless and out of work, they began to march about in the night led, it was rumoured, by a Captain Swing, firing ricks, breaking machinery and swearing dark, unmentionable oaths to obtain a living or destroy the Government.

> Ye gods above, send down your love,
> With swords as sharp as sickles,
> To cut the throats of gentlefolks,
> Who rob the poor of victuals.[1]

Their outburst, known as the Labourers' Revolt, was crushed with merciless brutality. The magistrates promptly sent for the militia. Two harmless men were hanged and dozens of others transported for life. The rebellion was stopped but the poor remained; and, by the end of the following year, every responsible authority agreed that soon something drastic would have to be done about them.

In the spring of 1832 Lord Grey, the Prime Minister, set up a Royal Commission of Inquiry to study the problem at every level; and almost exactly two years later he presented a Bill, based on its findings, which offered a novel and radical solution.

Instead of the existing method of relief, dating back to the days of Elizabeth, which cared for the needy on a parish basis and ordered the provision of family allowances, a system ought to be put in its place which would deal with the poor on a national level. The dole brought to the cottage would be stopped and relief instead provided in workhouses at a huge reduction in expense. Built on modern, scientific lines, under the control of a government commission, the workhouses would shelter the poor with care and economy. The needy would then be given a choice. Accept a restricted life in the workhouse with food, clothing and medical attention; or stay at home, find some work, and enjoy the benefits of freedom.

Amongst the people who opposed this scheme was, by a

1 *The Examiner*, 20th February, 1831.

stroke of luck for the poor and quite the reverse for the Bill's adherents, John Walter, the owner of *The Times*, a man, in consequence, of powerful and extensive influence. A Tory member of Parliament for Berkshire, a county in which he had bought a property at the very time of the Labourers' Revolt, and of which, therefore, he had first-hand knowledge, he disagreed in every respect with all the scheme's proposals. He disliked the idea of a central commission poking its nose into local affairs; he feared its wide and absolute authority from which, it seemed, there would be no appeal; and most of all, from the bottom of his heart, he abhorred the idea of workhouses.

To use the poor in a cruel experiment to prove that poverty was caused by idleness; to treat them as though they had broken the law, just because they were out of work; to lock them up like convicted criminals, just because they were destitute and hungry, separating husbands and wives and children, and even impounding their simplest possessions; he considered an act of truly monstrous wickedness.

During the passage of the Bill through Parliament which, in the Lords and Commons together occupied 28 debates, he spoke against it again and again, at the same time using his newspaper to back him up with letters, petitions and thirty Olympian editorials. Neither he, nor William Cobbett, another passionate defender of the poor who fought against the Bill as well with every means that he had in his power, both in the House of Commons and in print, had ever the smallest chance of success. The Government enjoyed a substantial majority, and Lord Althorp in the House of Commons with Lord Brougham in the House of Lords argued the case with polished confidence. They explained that pauperism had to be removed or else, within the foreseeable future, the poor would increase to such an extent and the rates would rise to such a level that the country would suffer total bankruptcy. A central commission had to be established or else the system would never work, and it had to be given authoritative powers or else it would prove entirely useless. As to the so-called Workhouse System, far from being a harsh experiment, in various parishes about the country it had been in force with great success for more than fifty years.

The Opposition mainly agreed, in spite of everything Walter

wrote, or every philippic delivered by Cobbett, and of every other protest and argument.

The Tory landowners and the Whig economists for once decided to vote together, the former wishing to preserve their property, the latter anxious to succeed with their plan, a combination of right and left which rendered all their opponents helpless.

Thus, on a bitter day for the poor—the 13th of August, 1834—the Bill was passed by a large majority; the Workhouse System was introduced; and all those who paid the poor-rates gained, in the establishment of the Poor Law Commission, a real hope of getting them reduced, and a new, drastic omnipotent weapon of authority.

Throughout the next eleven years John Walter and all his allies campaigned against the Poor Law Commission at every single opportunity. Whenever a case of abuse occurred they exposed the details as fully as possible, raised the matter in the House of Commons and demanded an open, impartial inquiry.

For a while it seemed that their cause was hopeless. Even the parting of married couples, the removal of little children from their mothers, the deliberate insufficiency of food, the unnecessary strictness of workhouse discipline, failed to stir the public conscience. As soon as the System came into use the paupers vanished as if by magic, and the poor-rate fell by twenty per cent. Naturally enough the public were pleased and not disposed to listen to complaints. The change was due to a surge of prosperity and not to the Workhouse System at all, but the Poor Law Commission reaped the credit.

Workhouses rose throughout the country like a chain of alien military forts, and the poor were seized like prisoners of war. Their protests were met with silence and contempt, and every effort to improve their lot was turned aside with scorn and apathy.

Then, on the death of William IV, the situation began to change. As Queen Victoria came to the throne in the year 1837 the weather broke, harvests failed, and so, too, did commercial prosperity. The country entered the 'hungry forties' with industry gripped by the worst depression that anyone, then, had ever experienced. More than a million were unemployed, and even in agricultural districts, not directly hit by the reces-

sion, the state of the poor was terrible indeed with all the
workhouses filled to capacity.

Every day in these years—literally every single day—in a
manner that then was entirely new, *The Times* continued its
battle against the workhouses: sometimes with only a single
item; often with a thunderous editorial; now and again with a
lengthy report on a detailed case of brutality or hardship which
one of its teams of special correspondents (themselves an
innovation of Walter's) had managed to expose in spite of
concealment; or else, selecting a wider target, against the
ruthless guiding hand of the Poor Law Commission in the
background.

In these seemingly endless years when so many of the poor
were starving to death or, in the name of governmental charity,
were locked inside their local workhouses, treated not like
Britain's sons in the proud tradition of 'Rule Britannia' but as
dangerous savages who had to be fed, John Walter's fight on
their behalf became a personal crusade.

He failed, in 1842, after a long and bitter battle which cost
him personally thousands of pounds, to prevent the Commission
being renewed; and once more for a while, he despaired. The
economy, however, got worse and worse, and Walter's chances
began to improve as workhouse conditions grew harsher and
harsher, the Poor Law Commission enforcing with rigour the
basic rule of the Workhouse System that life in the workhouse
should be 'less eligible' than anything obtained by self support.
The fact that work was not available, seven per cent of the population were simply unable to earn their living, did not for a
moment concern or deter it. Horrors came to light increasingly.
Week by week *The Times* exposed them. The Poor Law Commission tried to excuse them as mere minor administrative
lapses and boasted instead of 'gratifying progress'. Walter
maintained a relentless attack. At long last, in 1845, he managed
to bring to light a scandal of such a bestial and revolting nature
that, within a matter of months, it swept the Commission
away.

The events which led to the Commission's fall took place in
the Workhouse at Andover in Hampshire. The daily task of the
paupers there was to pound a certain quantity of bones, the
dust of which was used for manure; something the Poor Law
Commissioners had sanctioned in many establishments through-

out the country. At Andover, however, a special circumstance, the fact that here the Labourers' Revolt had broken out with more ferocity than almost anywhere else in the south, had led to especially grim conditions. The Guardians, a body of elected ratepayers who met in the Workhouse every week to decide on the paupers' claims to admittance had suffered, personally, so severely from arson and other acts of riot that when they found their former opponents suddenly, safely entrusted to their care they had not been able to resist revenge.

They had chosen as Master and Matron of the Workhouse a former sergeant-major and his wife who treated the paupers like dangerous criminals, and, with the Guardians' knowledge and consent, ran the Workhouse like a penal settlement. The Master, too, in the 'hungry forties', feeling the pinch like every-one else, had started stealing the inmates' rations. At the time of Walter's horrific disclosure, hunger prevailed to such an extent that fights had broken out in the bone-yard for any bone, how-ever stinking, to which adhered a particle of meat. The bones were mostly those of animals but some had come from the local graveyard, including a skeleton still complete which one of the inmates had hung on a nail. For a new church was being built on land adjoining the existing edifice, a number of graves had been disturbed, and their contents carted off to the bone-yard.

Facts like these could not be hidden, and rumours began to spread in the town that hunger had driven the inmates mad. As coffins trundled out of the Workhouse, watching urchins used to follow them chanting the latest popular jingle:

> Rattle his bones
> Over the stones
> He's only a pauper
> Whom nobody owns.

One of the Guardians, a Mr. Mundy, the only one who cared for the poor who had tried in vain to persuade his colleagues to make an effort to ease their privations, complained to his local Member of Parliament. Questions were asked in the House of Commons. *The Times* despatched a reporter to Andover. In twenty-nine dramatic reports, the longest series ever pub-lished, every aspect of the Workhouse System as conceived in theory by the Poor Law Commission and administered in practice at local level was stripped, at last, of cant and stood revealed.

Little remained for Walter to do but to let matters take their course. A Select Committee of the House of Commons reviewed the case the following year, and as, in the year that followed that, the summer of 1847, the Poor Law Commission was due to expire unless its term was renewed again it died, as it were, a natural death.

A Board was appointed to take its place, the Secretary of which was a Minister of State having a seat in the House of Commons to ensure a proper control by Parliament. Thus, at last, Walter triumphed, in fact at the very end of his life; for the week in which the Commission lapsed was, as it chanced, the week in which he died.

The problem of the poor, of course, continued; greater, then, than ever before as blight had suddenly struck the potato, part of the labourers' staple diet; so that no return was ever possible to the happier ways of years gone by when the paupers were helped by the parish authorities who had usually known them all their lives and gave them sympathy and understanding. The Workhouse System had come to stay, whether the paupers liked it or not, a modern, national network of relief, in keeping with the spirit of the 19th century.

The System was, indeed, the finest in Europe. It gave the paupers food and clothing, shelter, warmth and medical attention as a right and without cost, in every corner of England and Wales. The newspapers might complain if they liked; but the Workhouse System had been conceived by some of the cleverest men of the time, taking account of all the circumstances: the numbers of the poor, the distress of the ratepayers, the Labourers' Revolt, the uncertainties of industry.

Who could think of anything better? How, in a complex changing world, could anyone ask for more?

Chapter 2

ACCORDING TO THE Minutes of the Poor Law Commission, preserved in seventy-seven tomes, heavy enough in weight and content to crush the spirit of the keenest historian, the Commission formally came to life in the year 1834, the fifth in the reign of William IV, at noon on Saturday the 23rd of August.

In the quaint, ancient legal jargon which is always used in official documents and which, in this particular case, not only strikes the reader as curious but also seems to be far removed from the painful, immediate, human problems with which the Commission was soon to deal, the Warrant of Appointment certified as follows:

> William the Fourth, by the Grace of God of the United Kingdom of Great Britain and Ireland, King, Defender of the Faith, etc.,
>
> To our right-trusty and welbeloved Councillor Thomas Frankland Lewis, and our trusty and welbeloved John George Shaw Lefevre, and George Nicholls, Esquires, Greeting:—Whereas, by an Act past in the last Session of Parliament, entituled 'An Act for the Amendment and better Administration of the Laws relating to the Poor in England and Wales', it is amongst other things enacted that it shall be lawful for Us, Our Heirs and Successors, by Warrant under the Sign Manual to appoint three fit Persons to be Our Commissioners for carrying the said Act into execution; and also from time to time at pleasure to remove any of the Commissioners for the time being, and upon every or any Vacancy in the said number of Commissioners either by removal or by Death, or otherwise, to appoint some other fit person to the said office: Now Know Ye, that We reposing great Trust and Confidence in

your Zeal, Ability and Discretion, have thought fit to appoint, and by these presents do appoint, you, the said Thomas Frankland Lewis, John George Shaw Lefevre, and George Nicholls, to be Our Commissioners for carrying into effect the provisions of the said recited Act.[1]

The Commissioners took the Oath of Office before a judge, Mr. Baron Alderson who, as a member of the Special Commission which had tried the leaders of the Labourers' Revolt, already knew their problems well. Then they held a formal Board, engaged as Secretary Edwin Chadwick, lately Bentham's private secretary and thought by many of the Act's opponents to have been the author of the scheme itself; and ordered that every Clerk of the Peace in every county in England and Wales should be sent a notification of these appointments.

The public reaction to these appointments was, as might be expected, mixed. Generally speaking, in Parliament itself, they were broadly considered to be satisfactory. They were, of course, positions of patronage, carrying large and enviable salaries with wide and dictatorial authority; but given the fact that the habit of the times was always to offer such places as favours and never to fill them solely on merit, the Government's choice, being unpolitical, was thought to be fair, sensible and adequate.

Sir Thomas Lewis and George Nicholls had both previously dealt with the poor, the former in 1817 on a Parliamentary Committee of Inquiry, as well as at home, as a squire in Radnorshire where poverty was part of country life; the latter in actual practice at Southwell where, in 1821, he had introduced the Workhouse System, abolished pauperism almost completely, and reduced the rates by seventy per cent. John Lefevre had no such experience. He was, however, highly intelligent, was thoroughly used to government work, being Under-Secretary of State for the Colonies, and had served already on other important commissions.

The Times, naturally, attacked the appointments, praising the Government's cleverness sarcastically, calling the Commissioners paragons of wisdom, and three of the seven wonders

1 P.R.O. M.H. 1/1.

of the world. Events proved the paper to be right although, as it happened, in the literal sense. Considering the tasks that lay ahead and the skill and success with which they tackled them, the Commissioners' talents were probably underestimated.

The first of the tasks which faced the Commissioners was that of getting in touch with the authorities of every parish in England and Wales, of which there were nearly fifteen thousand, to discover the number of paupers in each and the manner in which these local officials cared for them. To each was sent a copy of the Act, a list of a dozen basic queries, and a covering letter intended to explain them. Questionnaires, tables and statistics were a passion with Edwin Chadwick, the Secretary. Very often it happened, however, that those people to whom he sent them, as well as finding them incomprehensible, were more or less illiterate; so that, in spite of his expectations and the time and care he had taken in compiling them, the information he received was of little use.

The subsequent history of the Poor Law Commission, recorded soberly in Annual Reports with innumerable sets of facts and figures, tables, diagrams, plans and sketches, is hard to convey with the passionate interest which, at the time, the subject aroused. Behind the promising reports and data that so many parishes had been united, that so many workhouses had been constructed, that so many paupers had been relieved, that so many pounds of the rates had been saved, lay another tale that was not recorded—a saga of misery, hardship and hunger told by the poor to each other in the workhouses—the truth of which, still today, with most of the evidence readily available, can hardly be believed.

Whenever it could *The Times* protested, and, as conditions got worse and worse, and more and more atrocities occurred, it exposed and remedied more and more of them; but, in the early years at least, when the System was only just beginning and proper control had not been achieved, wounds were inflicted on the working classes—on their pride and dignity as human beings—which even today, in prosperous circumstances, have never been wholly forgotten.

The outward facts can be given simply. By the third year of the Commission's life, the summer of 1837, the time of the death of William IV and the consequent accession of Queen Victoria, of all the parishes in England and Wales over which it exercised jurisdiction—a total of nearly fifteen thousand—only a thousand remained unaffected. All the rest had been formed into Unions of approximately thirty parishes each, in each of which the local authorities had been forced to provide a workhouse. Parish by parish, the reduction in the rates had averaged forty-six per cent. The total annual national saving had reached a million pounds.

Of course the Commission had faced some difficulties. Alarming riots had taken place, notably in Buckinghamshire, Bedfordshire and Devonshire, all counties of endemic poverty, all disturbed in the Labourers' Revolt.

There were two particular sources of protest: against the stoppage of out-relief—the provision of bread and money in the home, and against the break-up of home and families, both within the Poor Law Unions (the newly-established administrative units) and also within the workhouses themselves. In, for instance, the Amersham Union, one of the poorest districts in the country and therefore one of the first to be unionised, a riot took place in the parish of Chesham. Ten ancient men and a boy were told to leave the local poor-house in which they had lived happily for years, close to their families and all their friends, and were ordered to move instead to the workhouse, five miles away in the town of Amersham. A rumour spread that if they went they would never be seen alive again, and as a result a crowd gathered and attacked the cart that came to fetch them. Next, a local magistrate appeared and tried to explain the change in the law, but after being showered with stones and knocked to the ground by a man with a stick, he gave it up and sent for the Yeomanry. When they arrived they arrested the ringleaders, two of whom were the parents of the boy. Only on the following day was the wretched group transferred without disturbance.

As well as riots against such transfers of which there were numbers throughout the year, notably at Ampthill, a village near Bedford, for which the ringleaders were condemned to death although in the end they were granted a reprieve, there were other pathetic and different disturbances. These took place, in the main, in Devonshire in an area north and west of Exeter. William Gilbert, an Assistant Commissioner, reported one of them, unfeelingly, as follows:

Amongst other ridiculous statements circulated, the peasantry fully believed that all the bread was poisoned, and that the only cause for giving it instead of money was the facility it afforded of destroying the paupers; that all the children beyond three in a family were to be killed; that all young children and women under 18 were to be spared; that if they touched the bread they would instantly drop down dead; and I saw one poor person at North Molton look at a loaf with a strong expression of hunger, and when it was offered to her, put her hands behind her and shrink back in fear lest it should touch her. She acknowledged she had heard of a man who had dropped down dead the moment he touched the bread.[1]

Here, predictably, as at Chesham, the cry of protest was soon cut short. The local authorities sent for the Yeomanry and committed the ringleaders to prison.

Another challenge which faced the Commission, one over which it had no control and for which its instructions made no provision, was caused by pressure of the elements. In every agricultural community the weather and poverty are closely linked, and in 1834 and '35, open winters and abundant harvests reduced the numbers of the poor to a minimum and enabled the Commission to begin its work in abnormally easy conditions. Then the weather suddenly changed. The summer of 1836 was what, at the time, was called 'ungenial'. The autumn proved extremely wet, and after a perfect Indian summer of six balmy and cloudless weeks winter started on Christmas Day with the heaviest snowstorm since 1806.

Snow fell without a break for three days and three nights and soon enveloped the entire country. Every single road was blocked, every town and village cut off, and even London was totally isolated. When at last the mails got through and stories of the tempest began to circulate, some of the facts could barely be credited. At least fifteen thousand sheep were reckoned to have died on the Romney Marshes, many of the shepherds freezing with them. At Lewes, houses under the Downs were utterly destroyed by a sudden avalanche, with the loss of the lives of all their inhabitants. At Cuckfield every man in the

1 Second Annual Report, p. 353.

village was called to rescue the London coach which became
engulfed on the road to Brighton. The snow here was eight feet
deep, more than up to the horses' necks. Before it stopped the
following day, at least according to reports in the press, it had
drifted up to fifty feet and even frozen the golden cock that
lived on top of the steeple. Possibly this was a traveller's tale,
but reports which later reached the Commission in response to
a circular letter from Chadwick were clearly only too authentic.
For example, William Henry Toovey Hawley, the Assistant
Poor Law Commissioner for Sussex, duly submitted the following account.

Basingstoke, Jany 19th, 1837

My dear Sir.
   I much regret that a Tour of inspection into the Hampshire portion of my district, by separating me from some of
my most important papers, has interposed a great difficulty
in the way of my supplying you with so complete and
satisfactory a reply as I could wish to your letter (circular)
of the 18th instant, calling upon me for practical evidence
as to the capacity of the workhouse system to meet the
common exigencies of the winter, and the pressure caused
particularly by the late inclemency of the Weather; my
rough note book will however afford some convincing
proofs of its efficacy, which I will proceed to put you in
possession of in as plain and succinct a manner as possible,
with a hope that they will not be deemed irrelevent to the
purpose for which they are required.
   So favourable an opportunity as that offered by the late
severe weather for making an overwhelming attack by
numbers upon points which had hitherto been found im-
pregnable from an ordinary onset of assailants, was not
lost by those interested in keeping up the old system of
paying their labourers out of the parish funds, and on the
fifth day after the snow had set in, which was the Board
day at Cuckfield, no less than one hundred and forty nine
applications for relief were made to the Guardians of that
Union by able bodied labourers, thrown, as they alleged,
out of employment, and suffering distress in consequence
of the inclemency of the weather.
   To a few of these the Guardians gave a trifling relief in

flour as cases of urgent necessity, but to one hundred and eighteen the workhouse was unhesitatingly offered. Of these offers, only *six* were accepted.

On the following Board day sixty applications from the same class of paupers were made—every one of whom was offered the workhouse. Of this party five only entered it and came in on the evening of the Board day. The next morning I went to the house whilst the relieving officer was relieving the paupers to ascertain the final result of the previous days proceedings, and found that no more had come in—I also was gratified on learning that of the five who had entered it the evening before three, on being put to the Mill, gave notice of their intention to leave it, which they did before my arrival. The total number of able bodied men in the Cuckfield Workhouse during the frost was twenty, many of whom had entered it before, and of these, fifteen left it last Friday, the 12th instant.

This is the strongest instance of the successful defeat of a pressure caused by the severity of the weather which I have to adduce.

I remain

my dear Sir

most truly yours

W. H. T. Hawley[1]

E. Chadwick, Esquire
   etc   etc   etc

The snow, therefore, proved a success, at least from the point of view of the Commissioners. The worse the weather, the better the result. It had given the Workhouse System a test which all concerned had survived.

Less could be said about some of the paupers, many of whom endured the cold only to perish from influenza. As soon as the snow began to melt an 'epidemy' struck the country which cruelly attacked the snow's survivors. Mortality figures are not available, the registration of births and deaths being only then about to be enforced; but the rate of deaths of the inmates of the workhouses, at least according to the Annual Register, in

---

1 P.R.O. M.H. 32/39 q.p.

spite of official claims to the contrary, was the highest remembered for thirty years.

Hawley himself was taken ill—in fact he wrote his report on Cuckfield lying in bed at the inn at Basingstoke, hardly able to hold his pen. Probably supping treacle posset, one of the cures that was widely recommended, he soon enjoyed a complete recovery. Another circular arrived from Chadwick, and once again he took up his quill and supplied a cheerful answer.

It is my practice to take every opportunity of attending the Meals of the Paupers and inquiring from them personally whether any cause for complaint exists either in the quality or quantity of their diet, and excepting in one instance I have never heard any dissatisfaction expressed by any of those of the aged and infirm class: on the contrary they almost invariably acknowledge the excellence and sufficiency of their food, and are grateful for the indulgencies extended to them by the allowance of tea, sugar, butter, etc., and the only exception to this general satisfaction has been the complaint of a few of those who were previously addicted to drinking, that they are debarred the allowance of beer.

In most of the workhouses the comforts of this class are consulted by providing them with feather beds, and additional bed clothes if required. Some few of the very aged and infirm couples, have, through the recommendation of the Guardians, been allowed by your Board to live together; the workhouse dresses generally adopted are warm and convenient: cleanliness, order & regularity have taken place of the filthyness and immorality exhibited in the old workhouses: the duties of the medical men have been performed with the greatest assiduity, and that their orders for the supply of additional food, or articles of comfort required by the necessity of the case, to the aged and infirm have not been neglected by the Guardians, will in some measure be proved by the fact that in the Westhampnett [near Chichester, Sussex] workhouse during the Quarter ended the 25th Sept last not less than 174 Eggs and six Bottles of Port wine were consumed by a single pauper under an order from the Surgeon.

The shortness of the notice has prevented me from procuring intelligence from all the unions in my District relative to the second head of your inquiry, namely, 'The adequacy or inadequacy of medical relief as experienced during the prevalence of the Influenza' but in all those which I have visited since the appearance of the epidemic, I have found upon strict inquiry, that little, if any, complaint has been made to the several Boards, either on the part of the Poor as having been neglected, or on that of the Medical officers as being unable to fulfil their duties from the overwhelming accession of new cases accruing from the disease.

In one instance which came under my observation the medical officer had been attacked himself by the complaint, and the care of his patients was transferred, pro tempore, to two other medical men in the neighbourhood, to the satisfaction of all parties—this was in the Basingstoke Union. In all other quarters though the medical lists have been doubled, and in some instances trebled, thru' the prevalence of the epidemic, not an instance has come by my knowledge of any expression of discontent, or an avowal of inability to pay proper attention to their patients on the part of the medical officers.[1]

The Poor Law Commissioners must have been pleased. The Workhouse System was standing up even against the pressure of sudden disease.

The third and last of the Commission's trials in the first and formative years of its life was a Parliamentary Committee of Inquiry.

In February, 1837, after the snow and the influenza, and as a result of the countless tales of all the hardships suffered by the poor, the House of Commons, at Walter's request, set up a Select Committee of Inquiry to try to establish some of the facts and in general to study the work of the Commission. It began its work by examining a speech, made by Walter in the House of Commons, in which he had given various examples of the terrible cruelty of workhouse life. The first concerned the treatment of children in the workhouse at Fareham in Hampshire.

The Fareham workhouse had a large school to which, in

---

1 P.R.O. M.H. 32/39. 11th February, 1837, q.p.

B

1836, just before the snow had begun, three motherless, bastard children whose surnames were Withers, Cook and Warren, the eldest of whom was under five and the youngest only three and a half, had been sent for tuition by special arrangement from the neighbouring workhouse at Bishop's Waltham. Eight weeks later, at the end of January, they had been returned to Bishop's Waltham in such a weak and disgusting condition—one of them hardly able to stand and all suffering from acute diarrhoea—that the workhouse master at Waltham had complained.

The facts revealed at the subsequent inquiry held by an Assistant Poor Law Commissioner, this time a Colonel Charles a'Court in whose district Fareham lay, were almost beyond the limits of belief.

Once the children had arrived at Fareham, feeling upset in their new surroundings in spite of sleeping all together, one or all had wetted the bed. The usual punishment for such relapses was a cut of fifty per cent in the rations; and so, for a week, they had lived on the following:

	Each Child		
Bread	2 lbs	10	oz
Mutton		5	oz
Potatoes	1 lb		
Cheese		3½	oz
Pudding		12	oz
	4 lb	14½ oz	
Drink	3½ pints, milk gruel		

When they had failed to respond to starvation, they had next been made to stand in stocks, a set specially designed for children, in which they had stood throughout the meals which they themselves were not consuming. As they had gone from bad to worse and also begun to smell intolerably they had been removed to a shed in a yard in which they had lain together in a heap for ten days without a fire. At last they had seemed about to die; and so, to prevent their demise on the premises, they had been restored by the Fareham authorities to their so-called home in the workhouse at Bishop's Waltham.

In spite of such an appalling disclosure of what the System could do at its worst, fearlessly exposed by Colonel a'Court and publicly deplored by the Poor Law Commission which failed, however, to dismiss the perpetrators but gave them merely a grave rebuke: in spite, also, of other revelations, none so terrible as that at Fareham but many of them pitiful none the less, especially the hardships endured by the sick who, unless they came into the workhouses, had the greatest difficulty in getting treatment: the Committee agreed by a large majority that on the whole, and under the circumstances, the System was working as well as it could.

In fact, from the point of view of the Commission, its findings were little short of a triumph.

> Upon the whole, and speaking of those Unions to which their evidence relates, Your Committee are distinctly of opinion that the operation of the new Poor Law is satisfactory, and that it ought to be maintained. They entertain no doubt of the general wisdom and efficiency of its provisions. They think also that the administration of the Law has been, in the main, judicious . . . The authority of the Poor Law Commissioners has, in the opinion of Your Committee, and as far as they have had an opportunity of observing it, been exercised with great discretion. A more difficult task could scarcely have devolved on any department of government.[1]

So, in the summer of 1837, as Queen Victoria came to the throne and Dickens published *Oliver Twist*, the Poor Law Commissioners faced the future with hope and self assurance. They closed their third Annual Report by quoting a letter from a Mr. Woolley addressed to one of their Assistant Commissioners:

> I wanted to talk with you on the almost magical effect I find produced by the new Poor Laws in the South. There I had seen the evil in its 'riotings'; I saw no chance but ruin or change—prompt, effectual, decided, radical change; I began to fear the thing had been pushed too far, the remedy too long deferred; but I am perfectly delighted to find that I was mistaken. The change has been made, and the effect is more than anyone could have hoped. I have, in my

1 Select Committee on the Poor Law Amendment Act, 1837.

professional engagement as assistant tithe-commissioner, been much in Sussex and the Weald of Kent.

I have seen the effect on the poor-rates, the character of the population, the improvement of the land—such a change! I have talked with all sorts of persons, of all sorts of opinion on other subjects, and have heard but *one* opinion on this—that the measure has saved the country.

I am sick of the pitiful cry attempted to be raised against the measure, and especially at the supposed inhumanity of it. Let any man see the straightforward walk, the upright look of the labourer, as contrasted with what was before seen at every step in those counties. The sturdy and idle nuisance has already become the useful industrious member of society. No man who has not looked well into human nature, and the practical working of the wretched system of pauperism, can form an idea how different is sixpence earned by honest industry and sixpence wrung from the pay-table of a parish officer. I am fully convinced that the measure has doubled the value of property in many parts of the kingdom.

This is important; but pounds, shillings, and pence will not measure the value of the change in character which is already visible, and which I am well convinced will develop itself more and more.[1]

---

[1] Third Annual Report, p. 72.

Chapter 3

In the early days of the Poor Law Commission when, because the work was new, every act and every decision enjoyed not only its own importance but also created a vital precedent, none of the staff had more to bear or carried greater responsibility than those who were actually out in the field, the nine Assistant Poor Law Commissioners who put the law into practice.

The Assistant Commissioner concerned with Andover was Colonel Charles Ashe a'Court, already mentioned in connection with Fareham, whose district, broadly, encompassed Hampshire. Since he actually formed the Union, built the Workhouse and guided the Guardians, what he did and how he did it assumes a special interest and importance. First, however, a diversionary pause to look at the Colonel himself.

Born in 1785, the third son of Sir William a'Court, a Member of Parliament and also a Colonel whose father, too, had been a soldier, he spent his childhood at Heytesbury House, a vast and beautiful classical mansion, the family seat in Wiltshire.

Not surprisingly with such a background and also having to earn his living, being only a younger son, he decided to join the army. Due to the outbreak of war with France he saw active service almost at once, in Spain, Egypt, Italy and Sicily, in the latter place, in 1809, leading his men against an attack in which they took a thousand prisoners and he, personally, captured a standard. Then, with the peace, like so many others he faced a return to civilian life with little to do and less to live on. A letter he wrote to Lord William Bentinck, the Commander-in-Chief in the Mediterranean, to whom at the time he was A.D.C., expressed his fears with engaging honesty.

Palermo   March
25th 1815

My dear Lord William.

Notwithstanding what you mention in your letter, that you do not want me for the present at Genoa, I should immediately have applied for permission to join you there, were it not for an arrangement of a private and family nature, which has already so long detained me in Palermo. The fact is, my dear Lord William, when I returned to this country, I had no prospect but that of half pay and a pitiful retirement of some three or four hundred a year, without even the chance of getting further on in my profession & as little expectation of anything like a permanent establishment. Thus situated, I began to think that I might do well in throwing myself in the way at least of any aimiable person with sufficient fortune for us both. Connexions which I formerly considered as a sine qua non, now appeared to me but a secondary object. Provided the person herself were unobjectionable, it seemed to me to matter little what her parents were, when I could so soon separate myself from them. With this idea, after due consideration, and divers consultations with my brother, I formally proposed to and was accepted by Miss Gibbs. This happened early in February, and I immediately wrote for my father's consent: if he approves, we shall probably be married in the course of next month, & as I do not ask my father to draw his purse strings for me (a doleful and delicate operation with him) I confidently anticipate his entire approbation to my proposition. Mr. G. has behaved liberally in the occasion & even supposing me on half pay tomorrow, our income would not be much less than £3,000 a year. A portion of this however & a very principal portion, is in the shape of an annuity—a word I dislike, unless resting on solid security. Mr. G. & my brother are to draw up the settlements so that I am quite easy on this score.

As my father's consent is not *quite* certain, Miss Gibbs is very desirous that our intentions should remain secret. Even her uncle at Genoa is to be kept ignorant on the subject 'till matters are irrevocably fixed. She has unfortunately another uncle—My God what a man!—Patience

however—our acquaintance will not I hope be of long dura-
tion. I had a hard matter, in the first instance, to prove to
Miss G. & her father that my moral character was not quite
so bad as they appeared to suppose. I even authorised (a
bold measure perhaps) an appeal to Lady William on the
subject. It however required but a trifling exertion to
convince Miss G. that I had been wrongly judged here—it
is easy to convince a woman when she is only anxious to be
convinced. Her father's conviction followed as matter of
course; [*sic*] and all suspicions on either side are now, I
hope for ever hushed.[1]

The marriage took place on the 10th May, and, in spite of
Miss Gibbs' family, proved a great success.

When Colonel a'Court left the army he went to live at
Heytesbury House, his brother William, to whom it belonged,
staying abroad on diplomatic missions. There he remained for
sixteen years, looking after the ancestral property, taking part
in local affairs, at peace, surrounded by a growing family, only
disturbed in 1830 by the storm of the Labourers' Revolt.

In fact, at Heytesbury little occurred, but all around there
were violent outbreaks. Doubtless because of his military experience he was asked at once by Colonel Mair, the area com-
mander in nearby Salisbury, to do what he could to control his
district. The active, practical steps he took revealed the strong
and decisive character that all who knew him admired so much
when he worked with the Poor Law Commission.

The story of the Colonel's subsequent activities when he
joined the Commission four years later is, like that of the other
Assistants, an integral part of the early history of the Poor Law
Commission itself. From a suite of rooms in Somerset House,
three Commissioners, a Permanent Secretary, a group of clerks
and nine Assistants began to create an organisation which grew,
in the course of a hundred years, to the present huge government office, the Department of Health and Social Security.

For this particular reason, therefore, what they did, however
trivial, becomes at once of special interest. What, in fact, they
did achieve by sheer, dogged, persistent labour, must at the
time have created a record; one that many an office today,

1 The Bentinck papers, PWJd.42 q.p.

even supplied with modern equipment, would find it hard to equal.

As soon as a'Court received his appointment, on the 5th November, 1834, he was given a district in which to work, roughly speaking the county of Hampshire, and ordered to go there as soon as possible to make a preliminary survey. The Minutes of the Board record his instructions: 'The inquiries . . . should, in the first instance be directed to the following points: namely

1 The means of regulating existing Workhouses, and the extension of their effects and benefits to parishes in which there are no Workhouses.
2 The creation of Workhouses in parishes or districts where none at present exist.'

Working literally day and night, ten days later he submitted a report. He wrote first, privately, to Chadwick.

My dear Sir.

Every single sheet of my foolscap paper is expended & I have been obliged to purchase more. Pray supply my wants & send my despatch box if you can, addressed to me at Romsey.

I have worked like a slave to complete my inspection of this district. In confidence tell me if my mode of proceeding is approved of & kindly suggest any alteration in it you may think advisable. My work is sadly irksome: but if any good result from it I shall be satisfied. As yet I have been fortunate enough to persuade the several Vestries to adopt all the alterations & amendments which I have proposed.

The vote of thanks to me at Winchester is worth something.

In great truth
My dear Sir
Sincerely yours
C. A. a'Court[1]

Winchester
15th Nov
(1834)

---

1 The Chadwick papers.

Then he wrote to the Poor Law Commissioners.

> Winchester
> November 15 1834

Gentlemen.

The general bad management of the poor which I have found in this district, either as regards the workhouse system in operation, or that of out-door relief to able bodied labourers, can scarcely be exceeded in any part of the kingdom and calls for very serious consideration.

Whenever the workhouse holds out encouragement to the profligate—whenever it ceases to be a terror to him— whenever he courts its apartments and prefers them to his cottage and domestic circle, it is self evident that the comforts & conveniences which he there enjoys are far beyond his wants and greatly exceed what in justice to society ought to be afforded to him.[1]

Thus he prefaced the actual report which covered twenty foolscap sheets.

Chadwick thanked him, four days later.

> Poor Law Commissioners' Office
> Somerset House
> 19th Nov. 1834

Sir.

The Commissioners have read your report with very great satisfaction, and have pleasure in stating to you, that your activity and discretion in collecting the information which they stand in need of, are duly estimated by the Board.

> By Order of the Board
> Edwin Chadwick
> Secretary[2]

In spite of being cheered by praise, the Colonel wrote often to Chadwick, saying how much his work depressed him; complaining, too, like everyone else who has ever worked for a

1 P.R.O. M.H. 32/1 q.p.
2 P.R.O. M.H. 32/1 q.p.

government department, of the endless struggle to obtain supplies.

Lymington
Dec. 3rd. (1834)

My dear Sir.

Mr Cumberland [a clerk on the staff of the Commission] will go to Town tonight—pray let me have him again on Monday night. May I beg you will send my despatch Box to me by him—of which I feel the want at every hour of the day. I must also have a fresh supply of FOOLSCAP & *note* paper, but more particularly the former. I have been again obliged to purchase several quires.

Mr Cumberland will tell you that my life is not an idle one.

Very Faithfully Yours
C. A. a'Court[1]

B. Waltham
Jany 22nd (1835)

My dear Sir.

I am quite out of all sorts of stationary. Will you send me

Foolscap

Post

Note Paper

Perhaps my despatch box may now be ready for me?

Pray let the packet be directed to me at Petersfield where I shall be tomorrow night, if the Hambledon paupers will allow me to pass thru' their ill-fated village. I am to harangue them by appointment tomorrow. If they despatch me, let me have a Christian burial *at the expense of the board*.

I much fear I shall never be able to get on without Mr. Cumberland. For the last two days I have been obliged to work 16 hours a day to get thru' my work! If I find my duties do not diminish I must write to have Mr. Cumberland sent back to me.

I am getting heartily tired of and thoroughly disgusted

---

1 The Chadwick papers.

with my present life. I hardly think it will suit my views to be thus constantly separated from my family.

In great haste
My dear Sir
Truly yours
C. A. a'Court[1]

The Commissioners did their best to encourage him; and in reply, a fortnight later, the one with whom he normally dealt, John Lefevre, wrote as follows:

P.L.C.
5 Feb /35

My dear Sir.

I cannot tell you how sorry I am to perceive how much you are vexed at the obstinacy & ignorance which you meet with, but you should recollect that the greater these obstacles, the greater the merit of vanquishing them.

When you come to Town I shall be very glad if you can make my house convenient to you in any way.

Yours most truly
John Lefevre[2]

a'Court thanked him the next day.

Alton
Feby 6 1835

My dear Sir.

I feel greatly obliged to you for your letter of yesterday & for the kind expressions of civility which it contains.

Be assured it is not opposition that makes my present life sadly disagreeable to me. It is on the contrary the only amusement which my duty offers. I see however so much of the wretchedness of this world & so little of humanity & kindly feeling amongst the yeomen that I shall be heartily rejoyced to return to my own fireside.

Believe me
My dear Sir
Very faithfully yours
C. A. a'Court[3]

1 The Chadwick papers.
2 P.R.O. M.H. 32/2 q.p.
3 P.R.O. M.H. 32/2 q.p.

Two days afterwards he wrote again,

Alton

Feby 8th 1835

My dear Sir.

I will endeavour to be in Town on Thursday night, but as I am to have a public meeting at Alresford on Monday & another at Petersfield on Tuesday I hardly know to what delays these meetings may lead.

In the mean time let me *privately* add that I am heartily sick of my employment & will most gladly retire whenever I can do so without inconvenience to the Board. I am in truth but ill calculated for the constant drudgery I am now subject to.

In great haste
believe me
my dear Sir
Very faithfully yours
C. A. a'Court[1]

Another source of repeated annoyance concerned a cut in his salary. Almost before he had started his work, in the very week he arrived in Hampshire, he became aware of a Treasury rule by which, on becoming an Assistant Commissioner he was made to forfeit his military pay. Always inclined to be fussy with money, he wrote at once to the Poor Law Commissioners.

Winchester

November 6th, 1834

Gentlemen.

In reply to your letter of yesterday's date, I beg to acquaint you for the information of the Lords Commissioners of His Majesty's Treasury that when I accepted the situation of Assistant Poor Law Commissioner, I was in the receipt of my military half-pay of nine shillings and sixpence per diem, and amounting to the sum of £173 : 7 : 6 per annum. Under the Appropriation Act, I am given to understand that I cannot receive a larger civil salary than three times that amount without forfeiting my half-pay;

1 P.R.O. M.H. 32/2 q.p.

and that consequently whilst my colleagues are to receive
£700 as their salary I can only receive £526 : 12 : 6.

As I voluntarily engaged in my present very arduous
undertaking not on pecuniary considerations, but for the
purpose of aiding in the working of a great and most important National measure, I shall leave my case entirely
in the hands of the Lords Commissioners of his Majesty's
Treasury, and bow implicitly to their decision, be it what
it may.

I have the honour to be,
Gentlemen,
Your very obedt Servant,
C. A. a'Court
Col. etc., Assistant Commissioner.[1]

Bow, however, he certainly did not; but during the course
of the following months raised the matter again and again.
He did so, for instance, the ensuing summer in a private letter
to John Lefevre, to complain as well, with great disgust, that
the rule did not apply to the navy.

Fordingbridge
5th July, 1835

My dear Sir.

[He begins by referring to another problem, the non-
payment of his clerk, Cumberland.]

Whilst on money matters, let me express a hope that the
appropriation act may so far be altered this session as to
allow Sir F. Head and me to receive our military half-pay
in addition to our civil salaries. As I did not accept my
appointment from pecuniary considerations but from an
anxiety to assist in carrying out a favourite measure, I
should not have offered my observations as to the inadequacy of our salaries, had I not heard from the family
of Sir Ed. Parry that he has been permitted to retain his
naval half-pay whilst we have been called upon to relin-
quish ours.

On me this falls somewhat unjustly as I actually purchased all my commissions but one & have some right to

1 P.R.O. M.H. 1/1.

consider my half-pay less as a retaining fee than as a reward for 34 years military service.

Considering the station we have to hold in the County (& if this be not properly maintained, our influence would be nothing) the duties we have to perform & the expenses we have to incur, it is hardly fair that two Commissioners should be placed on a different footing from their colleagues. I do not wish however to do more than to mention the subject to you—satisfied that if a more equitable arrangement can be made, it will be adopted. I will only add that looking to my accounts for the last eight months & to the extra expenses which a separation from my family naturally entail upon me, I shall have profitted little more than 100£ by my civil services. I am quite sure that Sir Ed. Parry ought to receive his military [*sic*] pay—all I desire is to be placed on a similar footing.

> I remain, My dear Sir
> Very Sincerely Yours
> C. A. a'Court[1]

Lefevre replied,

> P.L.C.
> 9th July/35

My dear Col. a'Court.

[He begins by dealing with the query about the clerk.]

With reference to that part of your letter which relates to yourself, I need not I trust assure you that it would give me unfeigned pleasure if I were enabled to obtain for you a dispensation of (what appears to me a very unjust rule) regarding your half pay. In the course of next week I will make some enquiries on the subject, and let you know the result. I cannot understand the reason of the difference of the application of the principle to Naval and Military men. I think that if any difference should be made it should be in favor of those who have *purchased*.

> Ever yours Sincerely
> John Lefevre[2]

1 P.R.O. M.H. 32/2.
2 P.R.O. M.H. 32/2.

As well as complaining about his pay he complained also about the delay invariably incurred in receiving it. The delay was mainly caused by the Treasury to whom the Commissioners themselves complained.

Poor Law Commission Office
Somerset House
13th June 1835

My Lords.

We beg leave to point out to your Lordships that no supplies have been received by us or on our account for the payment of the salaries of the Commissioners, of the Assistant Commissioners, of the Secretary, the Assistant Secretary, or for the general expenses of the Commission since the 31st December last.

For some time past the Assistant Commissioners have been compelled to draw upon their own private resources to provide the current expenses of conducting the business of the Commission. At the present time they complain of being placed under circumstances of great personal inconvenience, and in other respects the business of the Commission will be impeded by any further delay in enabling us to make good the payments due on its account.

We trust that your Lordships will be pleased to direct the immediate payment of the sums we have stated as requisite for the prosecution of this department of the public service. [Approximately £8,000.]

We have the honor to be
My Lords
Your Lordships' Obedient Servants
T. Frankland Lewis
John George Shaw Lefevre
George Nicholls[1]

The Minutes record that the Treasury complied, the money being received a fortnight later.

Delay, however, was also caused, even when the money was there, by the Poor Law Commissioners themselves. When a'Court failed to receive his salary, still deprived of its military

---

1 P.R.O. M.H. 1/2 q.p.

increment to which he referred again and again until he drove
the Commissioners mad, he became extremely irritable. On
such an occasion he wrote to Lefevre.

> Devizes
> 30th Sept. 1835

My dear Sir.

I transmit my contingent account for the last quarter &
shall be *very glad* to receive the amount of it as soon as may
be convenient. I shall be detained here till Saturday & then
move to Warminster. If Chadwick could send me a cheque
on Friday, I should receive it before I leave this place. My
public meeting is to be held on Saturday at noon. I hear
that a clause has this year been introduced into the
Appropriation Act enabling the Lords of the Treasury, in
certain cases, to permit military officers in civil employment to retain their half pay. May I ask if this is intended
to apply to Sir Francis Head & myself.[1] I am quite clear
that it should do so, for I will venture to say that no men
slave harder for their civil salaries, & no men at the present
moment are more inadequately remunerated.

You may possibly find a moment to give this subject
your consideration—bearing always in mind that Sir
Edward Parry is allowed to receive his half pay whilst I,
who purchased all but my last Commission, have been
refused a similar indulgence.

> I remain
> My dear Sir
> Most truly yours
> C. A. a'Court[2]

> P.L.C.
> 3rd Oct /35

My dear Col. a'Court.

I think that when you have unionized Wilts you must
not attempt any other county at present, but content yourself for some time with hatching the eggs (a nest full) which
you have laid.

1 It did.
2 P.R.O. M.H. 32/2.

We directed £100 to be forthwith paid to you on account of your travelling contingent expenses. We expect daily an advance from the Treasury which will enable us to settle with you up to Oct. 1.

I regret to say that you have been so long from London that I have positively forgotten your face.

Yours most truly
J. Lefevre[1]

a'Court went home, and wrote to Chadwick.

Heytesbury House
Oct. 4th 1835

My dear Sir.

I sent my contingent account to Mr. Lefevre on the 1st inst. and requested a cheque for the amount before I left Devizes. It never reached me; & in consequence I have really been put to some inconvenience. May I beg of you to let it be sent to me by return of the Post to Warminster, where I hope to complete my arrangements by Wednesday night. The amount is £193 16s. 7d. for the Quarter, including the usual subsistence money of a guinea a day.

I really cannot be scampering all over the country without remittances. The 3 or 4 days which will intervene between forming my Union at Warminster & working up that of Amesbury, I shall spend with my family at Southampton. This constant separation from my family is almost intolerable to me. I am working unusually hard in this my native County, in the hope of seeing a period to my drudgery of forming Unions & of having a specific district allotted to me for inspection. Hants, Wilts & Dorset were originally intended for me. If each Asst Commissioner undertakes as much, the whole of the Counties of England will be amply provided for.

In great haste, believe me
My dear Sir
Very faithfully yours
C. A. a'Court[2]

1 P.R.O. M.H. 32/2 q.p.
2 The Chadwick papers.

Colonel a'Court's term of drudgery had, indeed, been extremely severe. By the time he left the Hampshire district in the summer of 1836, moving west to Somerset and Dorset, he had been in the Commission eighteen months, and had been away from his home and family for a total period of almost a year.[1] He had travelled more than 1,000 miles in every season, in every weather, at every time of the day and night. Dogged by the press wherever he went who noted every word he said for *The Times* and Cobbett's *Gridiron* and *Register*, he had made innumerable public speeches to explain the law to parish officials in every town and village of importance. He had built or organised thirty-eight workhouses for a similar number of Poor Law Unions, comprising nearly six hundred parishes whose population was half a million and whose annual total poor-rate expenditure was nearly a quarter of a million pounds. Added to this, every day, according to lifelong military habit, he had dealt with all his letters and reports even if, as he wrote to Lefevre, he had been compelled to work all night.

Lefevre, at least, valued his efforts. He spoke of a'Court's 'cometary course' and wrote, in a letter he failed to date, 'I have myself seen in my time much hard work, but I never saw such a long continuance of energy and diligence as in yourself and colleagues'.[2]

a'Court was pleased; also amazed at the great success of the System itself. He wrote to Chadwick in 1836, 'I am perfectly astonished at the working of the Union System in this County. The moral effect is surprising; and the pecuniary saving in all the Unions which I have as yet revisited . . . varies from 30 to 60 per cent. I may say that the saving in Hants alone would cover all the expenses of our Board and Machinery.'[3]

A last straw, as he left the district, had been the loss of Cumberland, his clerk, who had gone to bed and was 'breeding measles'. 'Owing to his illness I have had the odious drudgery of copying some 176 pages of foolscap paper in order to prepare the appendix to my annual report . . .'

The report, at least, was extremely good and was published

1 This is a guess; but it was estimated, officially, by the Poor Law Commissioners that Assistants would spend in the field 260 days in every 360.
2 P.R.O. M.H. 32/2 q.p.
3 The Chadwick papers, q.p.

in full by the Poor Law Commissioners, including a detailed account of affairs at Andover. The Colonel had been there the year before and had cheerfully written to John Lefevre.

Andover
15th June 1835

My dear Sir.

With the formation of the Andover Union, I have completed my survey of every parish in the County of Hants. I must however travel over my old ground at Winchester—Romsey—Christchurch—Ringwood & Fordingbridge—to say nothing of Portsea & the New Forest, before I can be quite satisfied that my labours are terminated. I have however been, at all events, safely delivered of my last public speech in this County for the Season.

Mr. Gawler, Mr. Dodson & Major Gardiner have been my firmest supporters here & kindly assisted at my public meeting this morning. The heat was intense but my audience separated in apparent good humour & with every wish to second my exertions.

Hereafter I propose to send to the Board merely an analysis of my notes in the several Parishes I may inspect. The notes themselves I cannot get on without. They stood me in excellent stead today and enabled me at once to silence incipient opposition.

In great haste
my dear Sir
Very truly yours
C. A. a'Court[1]

P.L.C.
19th June 1835

My dear Col. a'Court.

Accept my cordial congratulations on having finished yr inspection of the County of Hants and upon having with the exception only of that untameable part of the New Forest, combined the whole of it into appropriate Unions.

The Board have given their sanction to the Andover

1 P.R.O. M.H. 32/2 q.p.

Union, adopting the date you proposed & you will receive the order shortly.

Confidential. Do you know of any very good man whom you could recommend as a Cand[te] for an A.C.

Yours most truly
J. Lefevre[1]

a'Court's answer has not been filed unlike, happily, his Andover speech.

To Andover, therefore, in 1835 on a blazing day in the middle of June, to study the speech and his other activities, it is now incumbent to return.

1 P.R.O. M.H. 32/2.

Chapter 4

THE ANCIENT MARKET town of Andover to which, on Monday, 8th June, in the year 1835, Colonel a'Court made his way, lies in the heart of a farming district whose limits then, to the local inhabitants, were Marlborough, Newbury, Winchester, Salisbury; an expanse of down and stream and meadow as beautiful as anywhere in England.

An inhabited place for a thousand years, an area dotted with Roman farms, beside which, barrows and monuments record the passage of others before them, it had thrived as a place with its own identity, the home of several Saxon parliaments, for at least a century before the Norman Conquest.

Ever since, it had grown steadily, receiving a Charter from Henry II about 1175, permission to hold a November fair in 1205, on the Feast of St. Leonard; and from Queen Elizabeth, a Great Charter, which granted the right of incorporation, and established the celebrated Weyhill Fair, held yearly on Weyhill Down, at Old Michaelmas, October the 11th.

Here, during the 18th century, mountains of hops and cheeses were sold as well as vast quantities of sheep, sometimes as many as half a million, the early guide book, *Magna Brittania*, published in London in 1720, calling it the greatest fair in the Kingdom. Although it declined in the 19th century it was still, when Colonel a'Court arrived, a stupendous annual mart and frolic for which there were permanent booths on the Down—throughout the year a phantom village that suddenly came to life for a week. Sheep remained the principal item, closely followed by Farnham hops; but important, too, was the sale of employment, the labourer seeking his annual hire, garbed in the homely, comfortable smock, his trade announced by a symbol in his hat: a shepherd carrying a wisp of wool, a

53

carter sporting a knot of whipcord, a thresher displaying an ear of wheat. Swarms of gypsies, quacks and prostitutes added a touch of colour and excitement, and a pie-powder, or dusty-foot court, held by the Bailiff and Steward of Andover leased the booths, settled disputes and dispensed a daily ration of summary justice.

The sale of a wife in *The Mayor of Casterbridge* is said to have been inspired by a tale that such an event took place at the Fair, and the scene described at the start of the book may well be a picture of Weyhill Down. Such a proceeding, indeed, took place; but earlier on, in the town of Andover, in November, 1817.

Andover itself in the 18th century, apart from being enriched by the Fair, was a thriving place for other reasons; not only having a weekly market as well as its own St. Leonard's Fair, but also a busy trade in shalloon, a kind of cloth for lining coats, a fact noted by Daniel Defoe in the year 1724 when he passed through it on his tour of Great Britain.

A change in the pattern of the national economy which came about at the end of the century, and caused the downs to be put to corn and the woollen industry to move to the north, affected the local trade in shalloon; and in 1810 another observer, Charles Vancouver for the Board of Agriculture, reported the industry 'much on the decay'. When Colonel a'Court made his report the surviving weavers were out of work, the trade, then, in the Andover district having completely vanished.

The town managed to adjust to the change, principally due to its other industries, the chief of which was making malt; to its being, in 1789, connected by canal directly to Southampton; most of all to its geographical position at the intersection of six highways. The greatest of these, from London to the west, and those from the midland towns to the sea, brought thirty coaches through it in a day including the legendary Exeter mails which, in the 1820s and '30s, made the journey every day, setting off from Piccadilly and reaching Andover in six hours, a distance of sixty-seven miles. In the coaching era its inns were famous, most of all the White Hart, the posting house for the Devonport 'Quicksilver', the fastest coach in the whole of the Kingdom. In all, there were seven substantial inns as well as numerous smaller taverns, catering for hundreds of travellers a week to whom, in keeping with local tradition, the finest hospitality was given. Naturally enough, the town prospered; proving its growing wealth and importance with a new, classical Town Hall overlooking the market square, built in 1825 at the cost of £7,000.

Politically, it had just received its franchise, having been previously a 'rotten borough'; but its ancient, corporate government remained, its Bailiff, Steward and Chief Burgesses looking after it just as they liked.

These days were about to pass as Colonel a'Court came on the scene, and with them many another tradition—the banquets given by the ancient guilds, the ceremonial opening of the court, the jovial beating of the parish bounds, the exciting, bloodthirsty, public cockfights, the marathon exhibits of pugilism on the downs. Much fun yet remained. The annual ball in the Town Hall, held at the time of the Weyhill Fair, attended by everyone round about from the families of the yeomen to those of the nobility; mightily contested matches of cricket; delightful plays at the Andover Theatre; lectures on phrenology, astronomy and mesmerism.

Best of all, at least for the men, were the many social gatherings and feasts, nearly all of them regular events. Societies flourished for numerous interests—masonry, music, singing, horticulture—each of which had frequent meetings and each of which an annual dinner. The one for growing pinks and melons had been in existence for seventy years and the one that always met in August to eat a buck from Hurstbourne Park had started up in the 17th century; by whom founded or for what purpose except, of course, for pure gastronomy, nobody living in Andover actually knew.

If Andover itself was fairly prosperous, less could be said of the surrounding district—in particular of those parishes about to be grouped in the Andover Union—a number of which, not only then but even half a century before, had been submerged for years in abject poverty. Amongst these was the parish of Longparish, known to every sporting Englishman as the home of the immortal Colonel Hawker, and known, too, to every fisherman as being traversed by the river Test in which are the finest trout in the world. Here, in 1789, a local clergyman, Lascelles Iremonger, produced a series of actual budgets of various families within the parish. All revealed an annual

deficit. None could be pruned to make a saving of any kind
at all.

Budget of a man, his wife and two small
children, unable to earn anything[1]

Expenses per week	£	s.	d.
Bread or Flour	0	4	2
Yeast and Salt	0	0	1
Bacon or other Meat	0	0	4
Tea, Sugar and Butter	0	0	7
Cheese	0	0	5
Beer	0	0	0
Soap, Starch, and Blue	0	0	3¼
Candles	0	0	2
Thread, Thrum, Worsted	0	0	2
Total	0	6	2¼
Amount per annum	16	1	9
To the above Amount of Expences per annum	16	1	9
Add Rent, Fuel, Clothes, Lying-in, &c.	7	0	0
	23	1	9

Earnings per Week	£	s.	d.
The Man earns at a medium	0	7	6
The Woman	0	0	6
The Children	0	0	0
Total	0	8	0
Amount per annum	20	16	0

	£	s.	d.
Total Expences per annum	23	1	9
Total Earnings per annum	20	16	0
Deficiencies of Earnings	2	5	9

The price of bread at this time in Longparish for this family
was 1/0½d for a half-peck loaf.

1 *The Case of Labourers in Husbandry,* David Davies, 1795, p. 166.

Thus, only a morning's walk from Andover, long before the local enclosure deprived the peasant of many of his perquisites which happened here in 1804; long before the era of machines which did away with winter employment, threshing the corn as soon as it was cut; long before the Labourers' Revolt; long before the Union was thought of; many humble, working families had become dependent on the parish.

In the year 1795, that is to say, six years afterwards, due to a widespread increase in poverty not only within the Andover area but also throughout the whole of the south, a bench of magistrates at Speenhamland, near Newbury, less than twenty miles from Andover, issued a proposed scale of relief which varied according to the numbers in a family and moved in relation to the cost of the loaf of bread. They said, for example, that a single man should be given half a loaf a day (if, that is, he was out of work), the loaf being of 'seconds flour'[1] and weighing 8 lb. 11 oz. He should, if he only earned in a week an insufficient quantity of money to purchase this amount of bread, then receive from the parish authorities the balance in money to buy it.

By the Speenhamland plan the family in Longparish would have taken, weekly, seven-and-ninepence; a sum presumably held to be sufficient but one which, on Iremonger's figures, without extras, would not have been enough. Adopted throughout the south as a general yardstick of poor relief, it shows how close, even then, the peasant had come to starvation.

The labourer's poverty was next intensified, not in the Andover area alone but throughout the whole of the United Kingdom, by the astronomical cost of the Napoleonic war. As well as the rise in price of articles like tea, sugar, soap and leather, all of which were heavily taxed and all of which he had bought before but which, now, he was forced to give up, the price of the staff of life itself, the loaf of bread on which he depended, rose at times by one hundred per cent. He ought in theory to have received relief on a scale that would have enabled him to buy it and the price, therefore, should not have troubled him; but in practice he was given less.

The ever increasing cost of relief had begun to exceed the

1 Flour at that time was graded into 'finest flour', 'seconds flour', and 'thirds'. The finest made the best wheaten bread; the seconds made standard wheaten bread; the thirds made coarse household bread.

money available. Many of the parishes were nearly bankrupt
and so, too, were many of the ratepayers. The amount the
labourer received was diminished; and a bench of magistrates
sitting in Winchester in the summer of 1822, a year of excep-
tional poverty and hardship, marked it down by as much as a
fifth.[1] They used the same idea as before of pegging the amount
to the cost of bread but reduced the quantity given for the
price. Scarcely a scale of abundance earlier, now it became a
ration of bare subsistence.

Four years later, William Cobbett, in one of his famous
Rural Rides, published a description of some of the poor who
would then have been living on the Winchester scale in the
little village of Hurstbourne Tarrant, soon to be part of the
Andover Union.

> I wish, that, in speaking of this pretty village (which I
> always return to with additional pleasure), I could give
> *a good account* of the state of *those, without whose labour there
> would be neither corn nor sainfoin nor sheep*. I regret to say,
> that my account of this matter, if I gave it truly, must be
> a dismal account indeed! For, I have, in no part of England,
> seen the labouring people so badly off as they are here.[2]

> I went to see with my own eyes some of the *parish
> houses*, as they are called; that is to say, the places where
> the select vestry put the poor people into to live. Never
> did my eyes before alight on such scenes of wretchedness!
> There was one place, about 18 feet long and 10 wide, in
> which I found the wife of ISAAC HOLDEN, which, when all
> were at home, had to contain *nineteen persons*; and into
> which I solemnly declare, I would not put 19 pigs, even if
> well bedded with straw. Another place was shown me by
> JOB WALDRON's daughter; another by Thomas Carey's
> wife. The *bare ground*, and that in holes too, was the floor
> in both these places. The windows broken, and the holes
> stuffed with rags, or covered with rotten bits of board.
> Great openings in the walls, parts of which were fallen
> down, and the places stopped with hurdles and straw. The

---

1 Cobbett's *Weekly Register*, 21st September, 1822.
2 *Rural Rides*, 11th October, 1826.

thatch rotten, the chimneys leaning, the doors but bits of doors, the sleeping holes shocking both to sight and smell; and, indeed, every-thing seeming to say: '*These* are the abodes of wretchedness, which, to be believed possible, must be seen and felt; *these* are the abodes of the descendants of those amongst whom *beef, pork, mutton* and *veal* were the food of the poorer sort; to *this are come, at last,* the descendants of those common people of England, who, FORTESCUE tells us [in the 15th century], were clothed throughout in good woollens, whose bedding, and other furniture in their houses, were of wool, and that in great store, and who were well provided with all sorts of household goods, every one having all things that conduce to make life easy and happy!' [1]

Finally, before the Labourers' Revolt in the early winter of 1830, another cut was made by the authorities. From the scale of 1795 of half a loaf per day per man, at Weyhill, according to the records which are still preserved in the parish chest, the ration was sliced by fifty per cent—to one quarter of a loaf per day. On this scale by any reckoning, without extras of any kind—without money, without clothes, without so much as a cottage to live in—a man could truly hardly manage to survive.

Purchasing power of wages or dole of a single, agricultural labouring man per week, 1730–1830

In work at average wage *Loaves per week*		*On relief at average scale* *Loaves per week*
1730–1790	12	6
1795	6	3 (Speenhamland scale)
1822	6	2½ (Winchester scale)
1830	6	1½ (Weyhill scale)

The loaf being the gallon or half-peck loaf of seconds flour, weighing 8 lb. 11 oz. The energy value of such a loaf would have been about 1,200 calories per lb.

1 *The Poor Man's Friend,* Number III, p. 71. 13th October, 1826.

Parish of Weyhill[1]

Annual rate, shillings in the £	*Number of ratepayers*
1807 1/-	40 (First year after 1795 for which figures are available)
1822 3/6	52
1830 7/-	47

Principal landowner and ratepayer:	Henry Gawler
Overseer of the poor and collector of the rates:	Robert Cook
Population of parish: 1801	365 Census
1830	500 Estimated (by Henry Gawler)
Acreage of parish: 2,000	Estimated (by Robert Cook)

When Colonel a'Court came to Andover in the summer of 1835, after the flame of the Labourers' Revolt, he found the paupers utterly destitute. Those, that is, who were still alive: who had not in the meantime starved to death, who had not been hanged for their part in the Revolt, who had not been condemned for a similar reason to be torn away from their wives and families and shipped to Australia for life.

The Labourers' Revolt in the Andover area—the cause of so much that came to pass, as it hardened every citizen's heart and inspired a lasting spirit of revenge—erupted, possibly not by chance, on the opening day of the Annual Fair when the whole town was packed with labourers, most of whom were able and ready to join it. Accounts of what took place conflict, but every document still available conveys the alarm of those in authority. On the first day they maintained control, late at night dispersing the mob with a posse of constables armed with staves; but the next day, faced again by the same mob which had grown considerably and had fired some haystacks during the night, they had to admit there was nothing for it but to send at once for the military.

1 The figures for 1807 are taken from the parish rate book, at Weyhill. The rest are from *Commissioners' Reports* 1834, Vol. xxx, Apx (B.1.) Part I, *et seq*. State Paper Room, British Museum.

To The Right Honble The Secretary of State for the Home
Department. [Lord Melbourne]

Sir.

We consider it to be our duty to report to you for the
Information of His Majestys Government that numerous
Assemblies of the labouring classes have taken place in this
Neighbourhood.

The object of these meetings is to demand in a clamorous
manner an increase of wages—the destruction of all threshing machines and to require of the Proprietors of Land and
Tythes a reduction of Rents and Composition.

The practice seems to be to form local combinations
between contiguous Parishes to force all reluctant persons
into their schemes and to threaten an unison of Forces for
the accomplishment of their purposes. They also demand
and levy contributions in goods and money from the
persons whose habitations they visit.

Some threshing machines have been destroyed by the
rioters and some evil disposed persons have availed themselves of the prevailing spirit of discontent and excitement
to destroy some corn and hay stacks by fire in resentment,
as it is supposed, of some real or imaginary grievance.

It is our wish and intention to attempt all measures of a
pacific nature for the suppression of these proceedings
without appearing to yield to intimidation but we doubt
the sufficiency of the civil force without the aid of the
Military, which we should be reluctant to resort to unless
in a case of extreme emergency.

> We have the honor to be with great
> respect Sir, your most faithful and
> obedient servants
>   Richard Bethel Cox
>   Lucius Curtis
>   E. W. Blunt
>   W. Iremonger
>   Lance Green Walton
> Magistrates for the Division of Andover
> in the County of Southampton and
> residing near Andover.

Andover 20th November 1830

P.S. Since we wrote the above we regret to add that a large

body of the labouring classes joined by men of the lowest description have just now attacked and totally destroyed the Machinery belonging to an Iron Foundry[1] near this place & thereby created a damage to the proprietor of nearly or quite £2,000 as we are informed. The pretext for this outrage was, that the proprietor of the Foundry in question has been in the habit of manufacturing Iron work for Threshing Machines. We assure you Sir that the whole Town & Neighbourhood of Andover is at this moment in a state of the greatest agitation & alarm.[2]

To The Right Honble
  The Secretary of State
    Home Department
Sir.

In continuation of a letter which was addressed to you, in haste, from our Bench yesterday, we have now the honor to inform you that our meeting was attended by a mob amounting to several hundred persons from the neighbouring villages, clamorously demanding an increase of wages, & declaring their determination to destroy all the agricultural machinery in the neighbourhood.

Their expectations as to wages having been taken into consideration, we announced to the public our intentions in this respect, which seemed to satisfy the multitude who quietly departed forthwith to their respective homes, giving three cheers and 'God Save the King' on leaving the spot where we were assembled.

It is our duty to state however, that the success which has attended the proceedings of the several mobs in the predatory excursions thro' the neighbourhood has given encouragement to numbers of the most desperate characters to assemble together who compel the well disposed labourers to join them in their progress, and thus, as well as by their numbers and acts of intimidation, deprive us of the services of those persons to whom we should naturally look for support and assistance.

The focus of this gang is the town of Andover & we are

1 Tasker's Waterloo Ironworks.
2 P.R.O. H.O. 52/7.

concerned to state that after the parties above mentioned had dispersed this accumulated Andover gang returned into the town, from a long predatory tour, and thence proceeded at once to an iron foundry within two miles of this town where they destroyed the machinery moulds and other property to the amount of several hundred pounds.

We have reason to believe that this gang intend to proceed to further acts of violence tomorrow; & under the impression that they have the promise of support from a distance, we meet with extreme reluctance in all persons to join us in suppressing these proceedings; we have therefore deemed it our duty to make application to the commanding officer at Winchester for assistance in support of the civil authority in case of necessity.

We have the Honor to be
E. W. Blunt   Enham House
W. Iremonger   Wherwell Priory
Magistrates of the County
of Southampton

Andover 21st Nov. 1830

This letter is minuted on the back:

Ld. M. assures the magistrates that the Govt. is determined to support & assist them in this matter with all its power in putting down & bringing to justice the persons concerned in these violent & intolerable outrages.

Then inform them of the military force sent off to nearby —where sent & amt of force.

Add that Ld. M. relies on the united exertions & energy of the magistrates in resisting etc.[1]

The most violent fear was expressed by clergymen. One wrote to Lord Melbourne as follows:

Over Wallop near Andover
Hants. Sunday night
Nov. 21 1830

It is with the most painful feelings I think it my duty to communicate to you the dreadful state in which we are in

---

1 P.R.O. H.O. 52/7.

this Parish & Neighbourhood. Not a night passes without fires taking place around us. Yesterday a large mob six or seven abreast marched in regular procession in the face of open day with sledge hammers, sicles, axes and other implements in their hands for the avowed purpose of destroying a large Iron Foundry situated at the village of Clatford near Andover:—they effected their purpose without opposition—the proprietor's own men were even compelled by the mob to assist in the destruction of their master's property—although the proprietor offered 500 sovereigns to these diabolical wretches to spare the property—the loss of which is estimated at upwards of a thousand pounds: —tomorrow the mob have avowed their intention of visiting the village of Abbotsann adjoining this parish to destroy the remaining property belonging to the proprietor above mentioned—added to which we are all kept in the greatest alarm & agitation from the apprehension of our property being fired & the general feeling is that we are at the present left quite unprotected & at the mercy of a ferocious lawless rabble.

Neither life nor property is safe & at the moment I am now writing (—11 o'clock—) a very large fire is distinctly seen at the distance of not more than 6 or 7 miles—supposed to be from Corn Ricks etc.

I trust Sir you will not think me taking an improper liberty in addressing you on this most painful subject & I beg

to subscribe myself
Sir
with the highest respect
Your very faithful servant
Henry Wake Rector
of Over Wallop[1]

Another clergyman, Rowland Curtois, curate of Amport, close to Andover, seized the parish Register of Baptisms, a large volume bound in calf, heavy enough to use as a shield or to club to the ground a starving parishioner, and inscribed the following account of events on the flyleaf.

1 P.R.O. H.O. 52/7.

The 21st of November 1830.

This day will be memorable in the annals of this Parish. The Labourers rose in a Body destroyed every Threshing Machine & every other machine of any description & all cast iron work & demanded an increase of wages which demand was granted—the wages bein [*sic*] paid at 12ˢ pr week for able bodied Labourers above 20 & 9ˢ pr week for lads above 16. This rising was general throughout the County & there being no force to repel violence, all were obliged to submit to see the destruction of their property.[1]

A third clergyman, William Easton, in the parish next to Hurstbourne Tarrant, described by Cobbett as equally impoverished, whose personal payment to the poor in rates was only 5/2 per year, decided unwisely to show some spirit, and having safely ascended the pulpit, preached a highly provocative sermon. The next day the mob attacked him and extorted half a guinea from his wife. His son, however, recognised the ringleaders and managed to get them arrested at once. For on that day the revolt collapsed; at least, that is, in the Andover area. Lord Melbourne had taken action. The 9th Lancers had arrived.

The acts of revenge in the name of justice which were taken on behalf of society are still remembered bitterly at Andover and inflicted a stain on the Government's record which was equalled only once again a little more than four years afterwards at the trial of the Tolpuddle Martyrs.

One case will illustrate the rest; that of the men who attacked Mr. Easton. They were Henry Bunce, John Tollard, a father and two sons by the name of Sims. When they were tried, six weeks later, by a Sepcial Commission of Assize at Winchester, they had no counsel to represent them, this being the rule in force in cases concerning capital felonies; all the members of the jury were magistrates, that is to say, of the governing class; and three of the jurors had suffered personally in some form or another in the riots. The vicar's son, William Easton, a naval officer aged 35, gave the following evidence against the accused:

'I live at St. Mary Bourne with my father, the Rev.

1 H.R.O. Amport Baptismal Register.

C

William Easton. I recollect the 22nd of last November. About 8 or 9 o'clock of the morning of that day I saw a mob of 200 persons or more coming to my father's house: they carried sticks, bludgeons, pickaxes, and one of them had a draw chain. [This was explained to be a very sharp and formidable instrument used by carpenters.] I saw William and John Sims were in that crowd. I know all the four prisoners. They belong to our parish. Daniel Sims and Tollard were also there. The three Sims's had sticks, but Tollard had not. When they came to our wicket, they found it fastened. I went and asked them what they wanted. They said "they wanted to come in". I told them that they should not. They said they would. I again asked them, what they wanted. They again replied "to come in". I again said that I would not let them. William Sims then called for the pick-axes, and with a blow of a pick-axe the gate was forced open. They then came in and went to the house door. They demanded admittance. I told them that they should not have it. William Sims again called for the pick-axes. The door was then opened, but I don't know how. It flew back as if forced. One man then went into the parlour, and another went into the kitchen. When I got into the parlour I found William Sims demanding money of my mother. My mother said that she could not afford to give it. William Sims then said "Money or blood." She said that she would not give them any. The mob then cried out, "We are all of one mind; we will have money or blood." My mother then asked Wm. Sims how much they wanted. He said a sovereign. My mother offered 3s. Sims said, "We must have a sovereign." My mother said she never would give it. They again cried out, "We'll have money or blood." My mother then sent my sister Lucy up stairs for half a sovereign. I then went into the passage to the kitchen, and there I saw three persons surrounding my father. My father was that morning up stairs confined by a cold. I heard Daniel Sims say to my father, "Damn you, where will your text be next Sunday?" I then went up to them and said, "This is too bad. I'll mark some of you for this." Daniel Sims said, "You mark me!" and held up his stick at me. I replied, "Yes, I'll mark you." He said, "No marking." I said that I would.'

The witness was cross-examined: but nothing was elicited from the cross-examination, to shake the examination in chief.

Miss Lucy Easton corroborated the testimony of her brother. She heard W. Sims repeatedly say, 'blood or money'. He said that he would bring 500 more in the night, if it was not given; that money he had come for, and money he would have. The greater part of the mob cried out blood or money. Witness then said, 'money, mother'. She fetched down half a sovereign, and gave it to her mother. Her mother gave it to the elder Sims. The money fell out of his hands on the ground. When the mob saw that it was only half a sovereign, they said that it was not enough; that they would have more.

The Rev. William Easton stated, that when the mob first came he was up-stairs, owing to a cold under which he was labouring. On finding them in the house he came down stairs, and found his house in their possession. The first thing that the mob said to him was, that they would have their wages raised. He told them to go to the stocks, and there they would see, by a paper fastened on the church, that the magistrates had agreed to raise their wages. [See plate number 5.] William Sims abused him very much about a sermon which he had preached on the preceding Sunday, and which he said was against the poor. Witness denied that it was against the poor, and said that he had always been a friend to them. When he first came down stairs, he found his wife at the bottom of the stairs. She was then going to retire to her room, but the mob prevented her. She was so frightened that she could not speak. His wife had been in an ill state of health previously. In consequence of their violence she had a return of her former complaint, and was, as the doctor said, in a very dangerous state indeed for a week afterwards. As soon as it was known that his wife had given half a sovereign, W. Sims cried 'all out', and the mob left his house.

John Sims being called upon for his defence, said, that he had went to Mr. Easton about an advance of wages. Mr. Easton had met him a few days before and, in talking of these riots, had said to him, 'Stick to the farmers for your rights—that's the only way to get them.' Old

Mr. Easton said this to him in the presence of Thomas Young.

William Sims denied that he had ever called out 'money or blood' to Mrs. Easton. He had never got the half sovereign from that lady—a half sov. was put into his hand by that lady—he did not take it—he let it fall upon the ground. He would call a witness to prove it.

Daniel Sims.—'I did not hold up a stick at Mr. Easton.'

Tollard said nothing in his defence.

Henry Bunce was then called on behalf of Wm. Sims. Before he was examined—

Mr. Justice ALDERSON cautioned him very particularly not to answer any questions, unless he pleased, which would place either his life or his liberty in danger. Though repeatedly cautioned on this point, the witness consented to be examined.

Henry Bunce.—'I was present with the mob both before and after they went to Mr. Easton's, and whilst they were there, William Sims did not say, "blood or money". That expression was used, but it was by other persons.'

Mr. Justice ALDERSON.—'It is now my duty to order you into immediate custody. You were cautioned as to the effect of your answers, and yet you have confessed yourself implicated in this outrage.'

The prisoner immediately sprang over the bar into the dock with his former comrades, seemingly unaffected by the decision of the learned Judge.

Mr. Justice ALDERSON, in summing up the case, told the jury that this was a case of a very serious description indeed. He called their particular attention to it, as it was accompanied by circumstances of great aggravation. He hoped, therefore, that they would weigh the evidence with great attention before they pronounced a verdict of guilty, if such should be their verdict, against them. If they could only form one opinion regarding it, it was not the consequences which might follow their verdict that ought to deter them from giving it. He and they had both a painful duty to discharge, and must discharge it as became their duty to God and to their country. They must be satisfied that the money had been taken against the will of Mrs.

Easton—that it had been taken either by violence, or by apprehended violence to her husband's property—and then that the prisoners were all present aiding and abetting in one common object, before they could give a verdict against them.

The jury returned a verdict of *Guilty* against all the prisoners.[1]

Here the story might have concluded since all five were sentenced to death, commuted afterwards to transportation, and only two of them ever returned;[2] but it ends, in fact, with a shameful postscript.

Rewards had been offered for the capture of rebels—£500 in the case of incendiaries and £50 per head in the case of rioters. Mr. Easton and three constables applied successfully for £200 of which, having endured the most, the Vicar naturally took the largest portion.

The petition, now in the Public Record Office[3] (for the three Sims' and John Tollard: for the noble Bunce, nothing could be claimed) was made in July, 1831, and reveals the amounts that were given to each. The three constables got £55; William Easton was given the balance. The latter, thus, made a handsome profit, losing only half a sovereign and gaining £145. Considering all that his family had suffered—their lives threatened, their home besieged, and his wife's health seriously

---

1 *The Times.* 24th December 1830

William Sims married	aged 54	To be hanged. Commuted to transportation for life.
John Sims married	25	To be hanged. Commuted to transportation for 7 years.
Daniel Sims single	20	To be hanged. Commuted to transportation for 7 years.
John Tollard married 3 months	22	To be hanged. Commuted to transportation for 7 years.
Henry Bunce married 1 month	24	Sentence not stated. Probably as for John Tollard and the Sims boys.

P.R.O. A.24/18.

2 Probably. The register of burials at St. Mary Bourne shows that a William Sims, aged 88, was interred in December, 1862; a Henry Bunce, aged 53, in February, 1865. The ages stated here do not quite tally with those given at the trial; but few poor people in those days knew their ages exactly.

3 P.R.O. T/1.4193. Petition No. 11788, dated 11th June, 1831.

damaged—he thought, doubtless, that such a recompense was nothing less than reasonable.[1]

The rest of the rioters were treated similarly, especially those from the Andover district where more damage was done to machinery than in any other part of Hampshire.[2] Ninety-nine were sentenced to death, thirty of whom lived close to Andover in what was to be the Andover Union (not including the four sentenced for attacking the family of Mr. Easton) and thirty-seven got transportation, seven of whom were natives of the district. Only two, in the end, were hanged; all the rest were sent to Australia instead.

When calm came, so did reality, the hard pressure of economic circumstances, the inexorable law of supply and demand. Lord Melbourne rebuked the magistrates for having raised the labourers' wages, and once again the curate of Amport recorded the relevant local developments:

> At a meeting of the Vestry holden this 15th day of January 1830 [he meant 1831] pursuant to notice given on Sunday last for the purpose of reconsidering a resolution of vestry adopted 15th Dec. last
> It was resolved
> That the rate of wages of the able bodied labourers be reduced from 12ˢ pr week to 10ˢ.[3]

At this humble level wages remained for the greater part of the lives of the men who received them.

The gentry of Andover, flushed with success, in many cases also rewarded, though none so amply as Mr. Easton, received

1 Easton was Vicar of Hurstbourne Priors; Curate to St. Mary Bourne; Prebend in the Collegiate Church of Heytesbury, Wiltshire; Perpetual Curate of West Somerton, Norfolk. His total net annual income from these preferments including tythes was £542 8s. 10d. (Report of the Commissioners appointed by his Majesty to inquire into the ecclesiastical revenues of England and Wales, 1835.) He was a man of aggressive temperament, and sixteen years earlier had himself been convicted of riot when protesting, with others, against a service being held by a dissenting clergyman. He had been fined £5 and bound over on £100 surety. (*Salisbury Journal*, 16th March and 11th May, 1818). He died in 1834, aged 68.

2 Andover suffered 35 cases of demolishing buildings and machinery. Alton, South, the next, had 19 cases.

3 Amport Vestry Minute Book; at Amport.

permission from the Duke of Wellington to raise a troop of Yeomanry Cavalry which, to echo the words of its captain, Assheton Smith, a Member of Parliament, promised to maintain the district in perfect tranquillity. [See plate No. 1.]

As most of the gentry were also magistrates, and as all magistrates were guardians of workhouses, Colonel a'Court's arrival in Andover, four years later, to form the Union was met by all with profound enthusiasm.

Quite by chance it was a'Court's birthday, and quite by chance a travelling showman had arranged a dazzling display of fireworks.

From the very start it seemed auspicious—that the Poor Law Commission's plans for the Union were destined to prove a success.

Chapter 5

COLONEL A'COURT'S ARRIVAL in Andover was marked by a column in the *Salisbury & Wiltshire Herald.*[1]

Col. a'Court, one of the assistant Poor Law Commissioners, visited Andover on Monday last, and summoned the overseers of that as well as several neighbouring parishes, to meet him on Tuesday and two following days. The overseers underwent a minute examination as to the state of their accounts, annual expenditure, number of unemployed poor receiving relief, etc., and the capabilities of the present poorhouse of containing the requisite number of paupers.

Col. a'Court, in explaining his views on the subject, took occasion to advert to the demoralising and pernicious effect of the present system, and pointed out the advantages to be derived, both in a pecuniary and moral point of view, by the introduction of the intended alterations, which he exemplified by reference to the beneficial results already experienced in parishes where unions had been recently formed. The parish officers appeared to enter into the Colonel's wishes, and expressed their desire to cooperate with him in carrying them into execution.

The Colonel also wrote to Lefevre.

Andover
June 8th 1835

My dear Sir.
I hope here to unite some 30 parishes, tho' I foresee

1 13th June, 1835.

many obstacles to my proceedings. I hope however to secure the cooperation of *Mr. Gawler* & of the neighbouring gentry. I cannot expect to complete my arrangements for many days. Indeed if this intense heat continue, I shall melt away, before I can deliver my town hall address.

Very sincerely yours
C. A. a'Court[1]

He was out of luck with regard to the weather which stayed superb for more than a week, but in Henry Gawler and the latter's neighbours he found immediate adherents.

A month later he returned to Andover for the opening meeting of the Guardians. Of these, in all, there were thirty-six (not including any of the magistrates), one from each of the united parishes except Andover which nominated five, each elected for the term of a year by his own parochial ratepayers. Such a Board was much too large and could never have worked except in theory; but most of the Guardians never appeared except on this, the opening day and so, in fact, like most committees, it was actually run by those who cared, only a small proportion of the whole, and managed with adequate speed and decision in practice.

In a way that would seem amazing today to anyone forming a local authority, every single stage of the meeting from the opening steps to the very last were planned by the Poor Law Commissioners in London. Instructions, Orders and Regulations showered on the guardians like leaves in autumn. First, they had to be elected formally, according to a procedure prescribed by the Commission, to the satisfaction of the local magistrates. Then, they had to arrange a meeting at which three was fixed as a quorum; next they had to select a chairman, then a clerk, then a treasurer. Finally, they had to appoint the officials who bore the title of relieving officers to whom the poor in need applied. In each case, the duties of each were explained with wearisome legal clarity; also, of course, all they did had to be placed on record in a Book of Minutes. All of this, naturally, was necessary, the System being entirely new. Nevertheless, so much advice imposed on those so little used to it must have muddled nearly all of them terribly.

1 P.R.O. M.H. 32/2 q.p.

POOR LAW COMMISSION OFFICE
SOMERSET HOUSE, LONDON 1836
GENTLEMEN,

As many of you have been suddenly and unexpectedly called upon to perform the duties which have devolved upon you as Guardians for the administration of relief to the poor within the district comprehended by your Union, and as those duties are altogether new in their character, the COMMISSIONERS OF POOR LAWS FOR ENGLAND AND WALES submit to you the following explanations, in the hope that they may assist you in the execution of the duties of your most important office.

The chief, and perhaps the most important, officer of the Union is the Clerk to the Board of Guardians. The Commissioners, therefore, request your special attention to the statement of his duties, as set forth in the Rules[1] and Regulations for the management of the Board, that you may be fully aware of the necessity of setting aside all local feelings and partialities in selecting the fittest obtainable person for the situation.

The appointments of the Relieving Officers will next, in due course, be brought under deliberation.

It will be their duty to conduct the preparatory changes of the existing system of out-door relief. It will be their business to investigate the existing claims and all new claims to relief, and to administer relief strictly according to the statute, and in conformity to the regulations of the Poor Law Commissioners.

The qualifications especially requisite in these officers, as well as in masters of Workhouses, are diligence, firmness, and mildness, in the execution of their duty, coupled with a knowledge of the habits of the indigent classes. These classes are far more sensitive to the deportment of persons in authority, or to their immediate superiors in rank, than is generally imagined, and the manner of the rejection of their claims frequently affects them as powerfully as the rejection itself. Each of the Union officers should, therefore, be especially cautioned to be guarded in his conduct towards the claimants of relief; he should be reminded that it is his

1 These were published as Appendix 'A' to the first Annual Report, 1835, and form a book in themselves.

duty to treat the sick, the aged, and the infirm, with marked
tenderness and care; that a large proportion of the claims
to relief, which it will probably be his duty to reject, have
been created by erroneous impressions fostered by old and
vicious modes of relief; and that even the claims originating
in fraudulent rapacity will not be allowed to be met with
harsh language or angry deportment. He should, and indeed
must, so conduct himself as to obtain the respect and confidence even of the claimants; and he should be especially
apprised that the Poor Law Commissioners will visit any
instances of harshness or unnecessary severity, inattention,
or incompetency on his part, with immediate dismissal.
When the new modes of administration are once in complete
action, any tumult or resistance amongst the paupers will
be deemed to require explanation from the officer whose
authority is resisted; and a repetition or continuance of any
violent resistance or insubordination to the new regulations
will, of itself, be deemed strong evidence of incompetency
on the part of the officer who may thus have failed in
enforcing them.

The most successful appointments of relieving officers,
where candidates, experienced in the administration of
well-managed parishes, were not forthcoming, have been
from the officers or superior non-commissioned officers in
the army and navy.

The habits of firmness, self-control, and coolness, combined with attention and exactitude, imparted by military
services, have been found peculiarly to fit them for the
performance of the duties of relieving officers of workhouses, or of masters, with instructions.

The Commissioners consider that the observations upon
the appointments and qualifications of relieving officers are
applicable, even in a much stronger degree, to the appointments of the master of the workhouse; his functions being
comparatively permanent, and the strict management
of the workhouse being the pivot on which the beneficial
operation of the change, and the permanent working of the
system itself will turn, his appointment will be one of
corresponding importance.

Having, by the appointment of proper officers, and by
the arrangements for the reception of in-door paupers, and

the supplies of provisions by contract, provided the requisite machinery for carrying on the affairs of the Union, you will now come to the consideration of the arrangements to be made for the full and careful examination of the separate cases of all the paupers in each parish in the Union.

Some examinations into the claims of paupers, transmitted herewith . . . may, together with the occasional discovery of paupers dying possessed of hoards of money, serve as examples of the caution to be observed in such examinations.

Where the pauper is the head of a family, and he declares that he has no work, and proves satisfactorily that he can obtain none, either in his own or in any of the parishes within a reasonable distance, he may be offered temporary relief within the workhouse until he can get some kind of work; relief, wholly or chiefly in kind, in the interval, being given to the family, to prevent the necessity of immediately selling off their goods and breaking up the cottage establishment. The pauper should be distinctly apprised that such an arrangement can only be admitted as a temporary expedient, to give him time to look about him, and postpone the application of the strict workhouse principle, which requires that all the members of a family claiming relief should enter the house, and give up their goods and chattels of every description to the officers of the Union.

For the young and able-bodied applicants, task work of some sort should be provided, and the relief should only be given to that class of applicants in a form which none but the really destitute will accept. In order that the parish may be made their last, instead of their first resource, it must, whilst it shields them from the effects of actual destitution, be made the hardest taskmaster and the worst paymaster within the district.

The most convenient and successful mode of employing paupers of this description, is by the use of hand-mills for grinding the corn to be consumed by themselves and other paupers within the Union. In some instances, mills for grinding bones have been used.[1]

1 P.R.O. M.H. 32/3 q.p.

Thus the guardians received their instructions on these and scores of other matters in closely printed foolscap sheets, eventually bound into weighty books. Few, if any, can have read them all; and fewer still, as events revealed, attempted to understand them.

The Book of Minutes of the Andover Guardians, happily preserved in the county archives, records their opening meeting as follows:

FIRST MEETING OF GUARDIANS

At the first Meeting of the Board of Guardians of the Andover Union elected under and by virtue of the Provisions of an Act of Parliament passed in the fourth and fifth years of the Reign of his present Majesty King William the Fourth intituled 'An Act for the Amendment and better Administration of the Laws relating to the Poor in England and Wales' held at the Town Hall in Andover in the County of Southampton the eleventh day of July 1835

Guardians present . . .[1]

Colonel A. a'Court attended and took part in the proceedings.

Resolved that the Reverend Christopher Dodson of Penton Mewsey in the County of Southampton, Clerk, be and he is hereby appointed chairman to the Meetings of this Board.

That Hugh Stacpoole of Clanville in the County of Southampton, Esquire, be and he is hereby appointed Vice Chairman to such meetings.

That Thomas Lamb of Andover Hants Gentleman be appointed Clerk to this Union at the Salary of £60 per Annum.

That the Parishes in this Union be divided into four several Districts to be called by the respective names and classed as follows Viz:

[1] See Appendix A.

District No. 1	Population of 1831	Estimated population
Andover	4941	4748
Foxcott	72	95
Penton Mewsey	249	254
Penton Grafton	375	424
Appleshaw	372	356
Knights Enham	92	123
	6101	6000

District No. 2		
Tangley	281	283
Chute	525	501
Chute Forest	135	** (missing)
Hurstbourne Tarrant	850	786
Vernhams Deane	707	674
Linkenholt	109	87
Faccombe	276	290
	2883	2621

District No. 3		
Abbotts Ann	619	562
Longparish	812	775
Bullington	187	189
Barton Stacey	561	623
Wherwell	663	686
Goodworth Clatford	414	414
Upper Clatford	612	487
Chilbolton	359	375
	4227	4111

District No. 4	Population of 1831	Estimated population
Thruxton	246	269
Fifield	236	211
Amport	764	713
Monxton	293	276
Quarley	191	201
Grately	141	130
Shipton	286	287
Kimpton	387	383
Tidworth North	417	392
Tidworth South	254	217
Ludgershall	550	535
	3765	3614
Grand totals (not in Minutes)	16,976	16,471 (including 135 estimated for Chute Forest)

All situate in the County of Southampton except North Tidworth, Chute, Chute Forest and Ludgershall which are in the County of Wilts.

That there be four Relieving Officers for the whole Union, one for each of the above Districts.

That the Salary for the Relieving Officer of

No. 1 District—£90 per annum
No. 2 District—£80
No. 3 District—£80
No. 4 District—£80

That the appointment of Relieving Officers for the several Districts be postponed till the next Meeting and that Advertisements be inserted in the Salisbury and Hampshire Papers for Persons to fill such offices and that each Officer on his Appointment be required to find securities for himself in £100 and one surety in £100 for the due performance of his office.

That it is expedient that a Union Workhouse calculated to contain 400 persons shall be erected at or near Andover

1. Andover High Street, looking north towards the new Town Hall, 1834. Capt. Assheton Smith, M.P., is seen inspecting the newly raised troop of Yeomanry Cavalry.

2. Andover High Street, looking north towards the Town Hall and the new church, c. 1846.

The Andover Union Workhouse

By the King.

A
PROCLAMATION

Against lawless and disorderly persons assembled together to compel their Employers to raise wages, and committing various acts of outrage,

OFFERS A REWARD OF

FIFTY POUNDS

For apprehending each and every person so offending:

AND A REWARD OF

Five Hundred Pounds

FOR THE DISCOVERY OF EVERY INCENDIARY,

To be paid on Conviction by any County Magistrate.

NOVEMBER 23, 1830.

VARDY, PRINTER, WARMINSTER.

4. (*Above*) A Royal proclamation at the time of the Labourers' Revolt. (P.R.O. H.O. 52/11)

5. (*Right*) Notice published at Andover at the time of the Labourers' Revolt. (P.R.O. H.O. 52/11)

ANDOVER, HANTS.

At a Meeting of the Magistrates for the

Division of Andover in the County of Southampton, and also at a Meeting of the Magistrates for the Borough and Parish of Andover, respectively held on Saturday, the twentieth Day of November Instant, the undermentioned Resolutions were proposed and agreed to, viz:

THAT they would recommend the several Occupiers of Land, in the different Parishes within the said Division, to allow the Labouring Class within their respective Parishes, the following rate of Wages, that is to say,

EVERY able bodied Man above the age of 20 Years, the sum of twelve Shillings per Week.

EVERY able bodied Man above the age of 16 and under 20 Years of age, the sum of nine Shillings per Week.

EVERY old and infirm Person, the sum of three Shillings per Week.

THEY will also recommend that a Gallon Loaf of Bread and Sixpence be allowed to a married Man for every Child above the number of two, after such Child shall have attained the age of one Month.

IN consequence of the above Resolutions and impressed as we are with the Conviction of the impossibility of our Labourers existing on their present rate of Wages, WE, the undersigned Occupiers of Land in the Parish and Neighbourhood of Andover, are induced to agree to the above Resolutions, trusting that our Landlords and Tithe Proprietors or their Agents will meet us on Saturday the twenty seventh Day of November Instant, at eleven o'Clock in the forenoon, at the Star and Garter Inn, in Andover, to enter into such Arrangements as will enable us so to do.

John Sweetapple
Philip Henry Poore
Richard Fortesque
Henry Tredgold
Thomas Dowling
Joseph Wakeford
John Lywood
Robert Pickering
Charles Cheyney
George Guyatt
George Dawkins
Edward Ranger
Charles Holdway
John Reeves
William Longman, Sen.
Robert Porock
William Goodall
George Dowling

William Sweetapple
Samuel Guyatt
William Dowling
Robert Dowling
Abraham Goater
Henry King
Henry Cordery
George Dowling
Thomas Spencer
Nicholas Cole
William Attwood
John Holloway
Charles Mundy
Hugh Mundy
William Moon
Thomas Biggs
John Kellow
Thomas Hutchins

Thomas Longman
William Child
Mary Laws
John Young
John Chandler
George Chandler
William Chandler
George Young
William Leveredge
Susan Batt
Thomas Baugh
John Cole
Harry Church
Charles Church
John Herbert
William Moore
Thomas Sutton

Robert Longman
Henry Poore
George Murshment
Henry Simes
James Cole
Robert Tilbury
William Hilliard
John Knowles
Robert Tilbury, Jun.
William Cooper
Robert Martin
Robert Cole
Hugh Child
Ann Cole
Mary Farley
Anthony Kersley
John Hooper

Andover, November 23, 1830.

KING, PRINTER, BOOKBINDER, &c. HIGH STREET, ANDOVER.

6. Two photographs of the Rev. Christopher Dodson taken in about 1870.

7. Edwin Chadwick in 1847, from *The Illustrated London News*.

8. A miniature of John Lefevre. On the back is written 'Painted at Tunbridge Wells, 1835, by Cotton'.

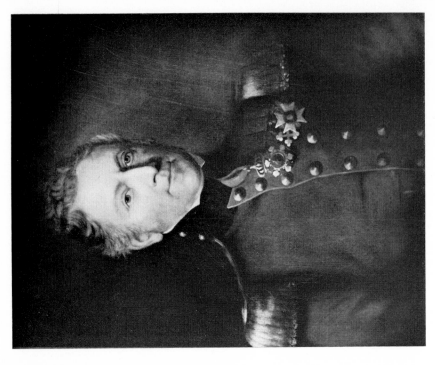

9. Colonel C. A. a'Court in 1837. Artist unknown.

10. A miniature of W. H. T. Hawley. Date and artist unknown. On the back is written 'Retouched at Limerick, Feb. 7, 1842'.

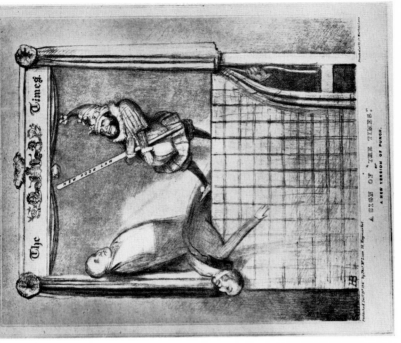

12. Cartoon by HB showing W. B. Ferrand, M.P. for Knaresborough, as Mr. Punch stunning Sir Robert Peel with a stick on which is written NEW POOR LAW. Sir James Graham leans, dazed, beside him. December 28th, 1844.

11. John Walter II. Date and artist unknown.

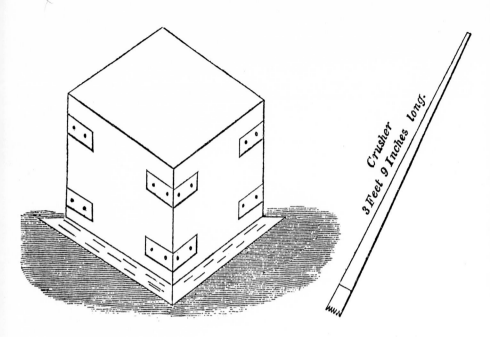

'The above is intended for a perspective representation of the box. It is made of inch and half elm, strongly bound with iron, and an iron plate on the bottom. It is best to make the top part moveable, so as to slip off from the bottom plate, which in some workhouses is fixed in the ground, and never moved. The crusher may be either all iron, or 3 feet 3 inches may be a wooden pole, with 6 inches of iron fixed on to the bottom. In the Beaminster Union each man breaks 96 lbs. daily, to pass through a half-inch sieve; but 80 lbs. is a more usual allowance. Some farmers insist on having the dust fine enough to go through a quarter-inch sieve, in which case a man can only break 40 or 50 lbs. per day. The work should be done under an open shed, and then there is no effluvia, or next to nothing, if the bones are dry. The bones are brought to the master frequently quite green, and if pounded in that state, they will smell, or a paste instead of dust will result. They should always be kept, if green, till dry, before they are pounded. The dust, if it accumulates in large quantities, requires to be turned now and then, or it will heat.'

13. Bone-pounding box and crusher as used in the Andover Workhouse. An illustration in appendix 26 to the Report from the Select Committee on Andover Union, 1846.

on such place and such site as a committee of Guardians shall decide upon subject to the approval of the Poor Law Commissioners for England and Wales.

That such committee be now appointed and do consist of the following Gentlemen, Viz: The Reverend Christopher Dodson, Clerk, The Revd Henry B. Green, Clerk, Mr. Northeast, Mr. Noyes and Mr. Baker.[1]

Before the committee had finished its work and reported the Workhouse ready for use and before, therefore, the Workhouse System could be introduced throughout the Union except in the parish of Andover itself which contained its own crumbling poorhouse, a number of ominous events took place which augured ill for the paupers destined to live in it.

The first of these, and much the worst, was Colonel a'Court's departure. In the autumn of 1836, having seen the Union created, having approved of its various officers, having provided plans for the Workhouse, and having, he hoped, found in Dodson an excellent, sensible, energetic Chairman, he handed over the Union to another. His last letters to John Lefevre, the last, that is, concerning Andover, tell the story in his own words.

Salisbury
19th August, 1835

My dear Sir.

My late progress to the North of Hants has had beneficial results, in as much as I hope I have stimulated the Guardians to much greater exertions in taking the preliminary proceedings necessary to the erection of their Work Houses than they were of late inclined to do.

At Andover I found more lukewarmness than I like on the subject of purchasing land for building. With the able assistance of the Revd Chairman of the Board of Guardians & of several members of the building committee, we at length fixed upon two sites. The one less eligible we know we can procure for 125£ per acre—the most desirable spot there is some little doubt about, altho' we offered 130£ an acre for it. The owner is going to give his final answer on Saturday; if favourable, well; if otherwise the other field

1 Hampshire Record Office, 27.M. 48/1.

will be forthwith purchased. Contracts will then be advertised for the erection of a building calculated for 400 inmates (the same number as at Basingstoke) on Mr. Kempthorne's plan[1] & the work will be commenced the moment your sanction is communicated to the Guardians.[2]

> I remain
> My dear Sir
> Most truly yours
> C. A. a'Court[3]

Southampton
Dec. 24th 1835

My dear Sir.

I have today rec^d a letter from the Revd. Mr. Dodson Chairman of the Andover Union suggesting that the proposed new Work House there shd be calculated to contain 300 instead of 400 inmates. I have stated to him that I am much inclined to agree with him in opinion that we shall probably require less Work House accommodation at Andover than was at first thought indispensible. Every day's experience convinces me that the new system may be fully carried out without the very serious expenditure contemplated; at the same time I do not think that it would be prudent to provide for a much fewer number than 2 per cent in the population of any Union.

Should the Guardians desire to build for only 300 paupers, they will officially request yr permission to do so.

Mr. Dodson observes in his letter, 'with respect to the Union generally I think it works well, though we labour under the disadvantage of being without a workhouse. The expenses of the poor in every parish are very considerably diminished, & the poor themselves are in many cases better off than they were before.'

> I remain
> My dear Sir
> Most truly yours
> C. A. a'Court[4]

1 The Commissioners' architect.
2 Final cost of building: £6,100; cost of site at £140 per acre: £600; total cost £6,700.
3 P.R.O. M.H. 32/2 q.p.
4 P.R.O. M.H. 32/2 q.p.

In May, 1836, Dodson wrote as follows to a'Court, the last letter he was destined to send him.

Andover May 2.
1836

[My dear . . . etc., missing]

The result of my observations as to the moral effects of the new poor law system upon the general character of the labouring classes in this union, is very satisfactory.

The labourer has now to depend solely upon his own exertions & is thus obliged to exercise habits of foresight & frugality, and above all sobriety, which under the old system was almost unknown. To prove the general improvement of morals, I will merely state that Beer houses have decreased:—illicit connexions & imprudent marriages have diminished. There may certainly be particular instances where the able bodied labourer is not so well off, when oppressed with a large family, as he was under the old system; but the general consequence has been to prevent wages from falling and in some instances to raise them.

Ablebodied pauperism has much diminished & is gradually lessening; and it must do so as a necessary consequence of the improved morals and habits of the country:—& when I say this, you will recollect, that we (the Andover Union) have not yet had the advantages derivable from the Workhouse system. The workhouse will, I have no doubt, wholly eradicate able bodied pauperism. Even without it the burden of the Poor rates has very much diminished, as you will see by a reference to the comparative quarters from Christmas to Lady day 1835–1836 which will be forwarded to you by to-morrow's post, by the Clerk of the Union. The old and infirm are at the same time equally as well taken care of, as under the previous system. But in addition to the advantages which it has conferred upon the poor, it has been equally advantageous to the moral feeling of those who are more fortunately circumstanced. I hear from all quarters that the current of private charity never ran so clear and unobstructed. I have heard many of the farmers say that they have now a pleasure in employing men who apply civilly for work; and who when they are employed are anxious to please their masters:—a conduct directly the reverse of the rude and insolent manner, in which work was formerly demanded as a right.

I have thus hastily given you a brief general sketch of the system as it works with us. I have written it thus hastily & without entering into details as you wished an immediate answer. Any information I can furnish at any time I shall be happy to give, and we shall be delighted to see you whenever it suits your arrangements.

The Workhouse goes on slowly:—there is a great difficulty in obtaining bricks, but I trust by the Winter we shall be ready.

> [I am, etc., missing]
> Ch^r Dodson

Expenditure for Qr ending Lady day 1835   £3,527. 4. 2d
Expenditure for Qr ending Lady day 1836   £2,149.17. 7d

Decrease   £1,377. 6. 7d[1]

Dodson's 'current of private charity' sounded fine to Colonel a'Court who sent it on to the Poor Law Commissioners who were so pleased with the entire letter that they published it complete in their Annual Report.

On the day that Dodson wrote it, however, he had also chaired a meeting of the Guardians. The Minutes reveal a tiny glimpse of what went on at the bottom of the charitable stream.

> Proposed by Mr. Goodall & seconded by Mr. Langstaff, That the present old and infirm Inmates of the Andover Poorhouse be allowed Beer with their dinners and suppers on those days when they have Bread and cheese only and that an application be made to the Poor Law Commissioners to alter the Dietary adopted by this Union to that effect.
> Amendment proposed by Mr. Northeast and seconded by Major Gardiner, That no such application be made which on being put to the meeting was carried by a large majority.

The diet in force in the Andover Poorhouse of which the inmates here complained was one chosen by the Board of

1 P.R.O. M.H. 32/3.

Guardians for eventual use in the Union Workhouse and it, too, marked a change which boded ill for the paupers.

One of the six approved dietaries issued for workhouses by the Poor Law Commissioners and known, technically, as No. 3. it allowed, unhappily, by some mistake in the copy sent to the Andover Guardians, even smaller quantities of bread and yet fewer rations of vegetables than those officially intended.[1]

Another decision taken by the Guardians, made before the Workhouse was finished, of grim promise to any pauper destined to beg for shelter within it, was their choice of a master and matron. Towards the end of 1836 they placed advertisements in various newspapers, one in London and the others locally, for applications from suitable candidates at an annual salary of £80; and after considering all the replies, of which they received exactly a dozen, they selected one 'by a large majority' and asked its author to come and see them.

At two o'clock on Christmas Eve, as the first flakes of snow fell, Sergeant-Major Colin McDougal presented himself to the Andover Guardians. He was forty-four, short and fair, with a slight limp from active service when his horse had fallen and crushed his leg. He answered all their questions well with just the required amount of respect and just the desired degree of decision. Mary Ann, his forbidding wife who had followed the drum for twenty years and given him three admirable children, made an excellent impression, too. They appeared, in fact, to be the perfect couple. The Guardians, remembering the Commissioners' advice in their first, formal, instructional letter that, in choosing a master and matron, a military background was usually the best, decided straight away to offer them employment.

The duties of workhouse masters and matrons were, like the duties of everyone else, prescribed at length by the Poor Law Commissioners. Much too long to be quoted in full, they began with a series of general instructions.

The following shall be the duties of the master of the workhouse:—

1. To admit paupers into the workhouse, and to cause them to be examined by the medical officer, and to cleanse,

1 See p. 86.

SELECT COMMITTEE ON ANDOVER UNION

No. 3—Dietary for Able-bodied Persons above 9 Years of Age

		BREAKFAST		DINNER					SUPPER	
		Bread	Gruel	Cooked Meat	Vegetables	Soup	Bread	Cheese	Bread	Cheese
		oz	pints	oz	lb	pints	oz	oz	oz	oz
Sunday	Men	6	1½	—	—	—	7	2	6	1½
	Women	5	1½	—	—	—	6	1½	5	1½
Monday	Men	6	1½	—	—	—	7	2	6	1½
	Women	5	1½	—	—	—	6	1½	5	1½
Tuesday	Men	6	1½	8	½	—	—	—	6	1½
	Women	5	1½	6	½	—	—	—	5	1½
Wednesday	Men	6	1½	—	—	—	7	2	6	1½
	Women	5	1½	—	—	—	6	1½	5	1½
Thursday	Men	6	1½	—	—	1½	—	—	6	1½
	Women	5	1½	—	—	1½	—	—	5	1½
Friday	Men	6	1½	—	—	—	7	2	6	1½
	Women	5	1½	—	—	—	6	1½	5	1½
Saturday	Men	6	1½	Bacon: 5	½	—	—	—	6	1½
	Women	5	1½	4	½	—	—	—	5	1½

Old people of 60 years of age and upwards may be allowed 1 oz of tea, 7 oz of butter, and 8 oz of sugar per week, in lieu of gruel for breakfast, if deemed expedient to make this change.

Children under 9 years of age to be dieted at discretion; above 9 to be allowed the same quantities as women.

Sick to be dieted as directed by the medical officer.

clothe, and place them in the proper wards, according to the regulations herein established.

2. To enforce industry, order, punctuality, and cleanliness, and the observance of the several rules herein contained, by the paupers in the workhouse, and by the several officers, servants, and other persons therein employed.

3. To read prayers to the paupers before breakfast and after supper every day, or cause them to be read, at which all the inmates must attend; but if any of the paupers shall profess religious principles indisposing them to unite in such service, they are to be permitted to sit apart, and not to be compelled to join in the same.

4. To inspect and call over the names of all the paupers immediately after morning prayers every day, and see that each individual is clean, and in a proper state.

5. To provide for and enforce the employment of the able-bodied adult paupers during the whole of the hours of labour; to train the youth in such employment as will best fit them for service; to keep the partially disabled paupers occupied to the extent of their ability; and to leave none who are capable of employment idle at any time.

6. To visit the sleeping wards of the first, second, and third classes at 11 o'clock every day, to see that they have been all duly cleaned and propery ventilated.

7. To see that the meals of the paupers are properly dressed and served, and to superintend the distribution thereof.

8. To say or cause to be said grace before and after meals.

9. To see that the dining halls, tables, and seats, are cleaned after each meal.

10. To visit all the wards of the male paupers at nine o'clock every night, and see that all the male paupers are in bed, and that all fires and lights are extinguished.

11. To receive from the gatekeeper the keys of the workhouse at nine o'clock every night, and to deliver them to him again at six o'clock every morning.

The following shall be the duties of the matron of the workhouse:—

1. To see that the in-door work of the establishment is,

as far as possible, performed by the female paupers maintained therein.

2. To provide for and enforce the employment of the able-bodied female paupers during the whole of the hours of labour; and to keep the partially disabled paupers occupied to the extent of their ability.

3. To visit all the wards of the females and children every night, and to ascertain that all the paupers in such wards are in bed, and the fires and lights duly extinguished.

4. To pay particular attention to the moral conduct and orderly behaviour of the female paupers and children; to see that they are clean and decent in their dress and persons, and to train them up in such employments as will best fit them for service.

5. To superintend and give the necessary directions for making and mending the clothing supplied to the female paupers and pauper children; and also the linen supplied to the male paupers of the Union; and to take care that all such clothing or linen be marked with the name of the Union.

6. To see that every pauper in the workhouse has clean linen and stockings once a week, and that all the beds be supplied with clean sheets once a month.

7. To take charge of the linen and stockings for the use of the paupers, and any other linen in use in the house, and to superintend and give the necessary directions concerning the washing, drying, and getting up the same, and not to permit any to be dried in the sleeping wards, or in the sick or lunatic wards.

8. To take care, with the assistance of the nurses, of the sick paupers and young children in the workhouse; to see that they are clean in their persons, and to provide such diet for the sick paupers and the young children as the medical officer shall direct, and to furnish them with such changes of clothes and linen as may be necessary.

9. To assist the master in the general management and superintendence of the workhouse, and especially in

Enforcing the observance of good order, cleanliness, punctuality, industry, and decency of demeanour among the paupers.

The cleansing and clothing of female paupers on their admission.

The cleansing and ventilating the sleeping wards and the dining halls, and all parts of the premises.

The placing in store and taking charge of the provisions, clothing and linen belonging to the Union.

10. And generally to observe and fulfil all lawful orders and directions of the board of guardians, and the rules, orders and regulations issued by the Poor Law Commissioners.[1]

The final, ominous event for the paupers, already noted earlier on, was Colonel a'Court's departure.

However much, when he came to Andover, he had truly believed in the Workhouse System; however much, as the Union progressed, he had urged obedience to the Poor Law Commissioners; and however much his military approach had led to the paupers being dragooned, his strict, upright soldierly character had also led to their being protected. When he left he was followed by Hawley who was still the Assistant Commissioner for Sussex, and soon to show his temperament at Cuckfield. From that moment, the Andover paupers were doomed.

William Henry Toovey Hawley superficially resembled a'Court in that he came from a military family and in that he lived in a beautiful house and was therefore a member of the class that is generally described as landed gentry. Here, as the paupers soon discovered, the likeness abruptly ended. Born in 1794 (slightly younger, therefore, than the Colonel) he was heir to a charming family property in the Hampshire village of Hartley Wintney—now in the possession of the National Trust —known as West Green House. His great-grandfather was 'Hangman Hawley', the notorious general under Cumberland who had butchered the Jacobites after Culloden and who, it was often privately alleged, was a natural son of George II. Like his sire who had built the house with all the taste and style of the age, Hawley adopted an elegant life. He shot, hunted, fished and raced, could draw well, and write verses—the last not particularly clever but proof, at least, of a cultivated mind.

1 First Annual Report, p. 101.

Like his sire he was also promiscuous. Twenty-two illegitimate heirs are said to have sprung from 'Hangman Hawley'; and Hawley, also legally childless, left an acknowledged natural family. Like the general, worst of all, whether as a member of the Yeomanry Cavalry, whether as a Justice of the Peace in court or whether as an Assistant Poor Law Commissioner, he enforced the letter of the law with heartless severity.

His early life is wrapped in obscurity. Apart from going to school at Winchester and then serving with an infantry regiment which he left probably in 1820, and apart from marrying his first cousin, a Miss Broughton, in 1821, a marriage that proved unhappy and barren, little else is recorded at all until he became an Assistant Commissioner in November, 1834.

His appointment happened to be the last, all the others having been made, and quite possibly it had caused the Commissioners a certain amount of difficulty. *The Times*, at any rate, remarked sardonically:[1]

> The Central Board has hatched its brood of assistant commissioners. The round dozen of prodigies of wisdom is all but complete. Eight little wonders of the world are now produced by the three prime phoenixes—eight chips of the block, eight sons of the board—can the universe furnish a ninth? Yes, it is said that the phoenixes are now sitting on a ninth egg. May it not be addled.

A bad egg, in many ways, William Henry Toovey Hawley certainly proved to be.

Hawley's opening move at Andover to which he came in 1836 is proudly recalled in the letter to Chadwick, part of which has been quoted already concerning the paupers at Cuckfield. Chadwick had asked him about the snow and how it had affected the Workhouse System. Hawley described it at Andover as follows, writing in January, 1837, immediately after McDougal's appointment.

> The first instance, which has practically come under my observation, of the abettors of the old system endeavour-

ing, on the approach of Winter, to re-establish its abuses, was in the well-managed Union at Andover.

At their Board day on the 24th September last fifteen able-bodied Paupers made their appearance, the first who had been thrown out of employment in consequence of the cessation of their autumnal labours in the harvest field. These men all came from *one* parish notorious for its pauperism: the parish of Longparish, and as it was the first occasion, at that period of the year, on which the Guardians had been called upon to deal with cases of this description, and as the Rule for prohibiting outdoor relief to the able bodied paupers had not yet been applied to their Union, they requested my advice how to act.

Foreseeing the danger there would be in setting a precedent for giving out-door relief in such cases, I soon relieved them from their difficulty by recommending them to offer the whole of them, with their families, the Workhouse. [He means the Andover parish poorhouse.] The advice was taken, and I requested the Chairman to let me know the result. A letter from him written on their next Board-day, informed me that *not one* had taken advantage of the offer—that thirteen had procured employment in their own parish from the farmers, and that the remaining two had got work on the roads (also in the parish) at the full wages of the District. A different course of proceeding would have saddled the parish with the support of these families during the whole winter.

This practical effect of the Workhouse applied as a test of the real destitution of the Parties claiming relief, instantly opened the Eyes of the Guardians, and during the period which had elapsed since the visit I now speak of, and one which I paid them subsequently on the 3rd December last, I found that orders for the house had been issued to upwards of *four hundred paupers,* only seven of whom had accepted them.[1]

Thus, at the start of 1837, all was set, at least in Andover, to extinguish the national curse of pauperism by the simple method of the Workhouse System.

1 P.R.O. M.H. 32/39. 19th January, 1837.

The Guardians were frankly pleased with the prospect, and
when the System came under attack, both in Parliament and
in the newspapers because of its failure during the snow, as
they themselves had declined relief to every single pauper who
applied,[1] they decided to advise the Poor Law Commissioners
that they, at least, approved of it. A meeting held on the 4th
February is reported in the Minutes as follows:

> Resolved by a large majority of this meeting that a
> copy of the following Resolutions be signed by the Clerk
> on behalf of the Guardians and forwarded to the Poor
> Law Commissioners.
> 1st That this Board have much satisfaction in observing
> the beneficial Results of the Poor Law Amendment Act.
> 2[d] That throughout this Union there is not a single
> instance of any able bodied Man receiving Relief for
> insufficiency of earnings though the pay of the Old Infirm
> and really destitute is still continued to them and generally
> speaking increased.
> 3[d] That in every District of this Union there are favorable
> symptoms of returning Industry and good Conduct as
> proofs of which many Parishes have had no cause for
> Magisterial interference since the Law came into operation
> and the relative feelings of Employers and Labourers are
> improved towards each other.
> 4th That these great advantages have chiefly sprung from
> the Workhouse System which is as necessary to guard the
> Industrious against the corrupting influence of Parish
> Relief as to guard the Parish against the idle and the
> fraudulent.
> 5th That this Board feel and acknowledge the benefit of
> being under the control and direction of the Central Board
> a tribunal divested of local interests and party passion
> and of the occasional presence of an Assistant Commis-
> sioner to aid them with his experience and advice.
> 6th That this Board deem it their duty to make this declara-
> tion of their sentiments in consequence of statements made

---

1 Hawley to the Poor Law Commissioners 8th February, 1837. Andover
was given as an example of one of the Unions in which 'no relief whatever
was given to the able bodied paupers on the occasion of the severity of
the weather'.

by the Opponents of this measure, statements which their own experience convinces them are utterly at variance with fair and sound principles.

On the above Resolution being read to the Meeting Mr. Hugh Mundy and Mr. James Baker, two of the Guardians for Andover severally entered their protest against them the latter not as condemning the Poor Law Amendment Act of the salutary effects of which he highly approved but as objecting to the manner in which its provisions have been carried into effect by the Guardians of this Union.

Mr. Mundy objected to them all. As the years went by he protested frequently. As yet, however, he spoke alone—his time was still to come.

Workhouse Orders and Regulations were, like other documents of guidance, compiled and printed by the Poor Law Commissioners in the greatest detail and length. Published in the first Annual Report but far too long to be quoted here, they contained, in part, the following:

Orders and Regulations to be observed in the Workhouse of the.......................Union.

I. PAUPERS are to be admitted into the workhouse in any one of the following modes, and in no other; viz.—

By an order of the board of guardians, signified in writing by their clerk.

By a provisional order in writing, signed by an overseer, churchwarden or relieving officer.

By the master of the workhouse, without any such order, in case of any sudden or urgent necessity.

IV. As soon as a pauper is admitted, he or she shall be placed in the probationary ward, and shall there remain until examined by the medical officer of the workhouse.

VII. Before removal from the probationary ward, the pauper shall be thoroughly cleansed, and shall be clothed in the workhouse dress; and the clothes which he or she wore upon admission shall be purified and deposited in a place to be appropriated for that purpose, to be restored to the pauper on leaving the workhouse, or else to be used by the pauper as the Board of Guardians shall direct.

Classification of paupers

IX. The in-door paupers shall be classed as follows:—
1. Aged or infirm men.
2. Able-bodied men, and youths above 13.
3. Youths and boys above 7 years old and under 13.
4. Aged or infirm women.
5. Able-bodied women, and girls above 16.
6. Girls above seven years of age and under 16.
7. Children under seven years of age.

X. To each class shall be assigned by the board of guardians that apartment or separate building which may be best fitted for the reception of such class, and in which they shall respectively remain, without communication, unless as is hereinafter provided.

Discipline and Diet

XIII. All the paupers in the workhouse, except the sick, the aged and infirm, and the young children, shall rise, be set to work, leave off work, and go to bed, at the times mentioned in the accompanying table 'A',[1] and shall be allowed such intervals for their meals as therein are stated; and these several times shall be notified by ringing a bell, and during the time of meals, silence, order and decorum shall be maintained.

XIV. Half an hour after the bell shall have been rung for rising, the names shall be called over in the several wards provided for the second, third, fifth and sixth classes, when every pauper belonging to the ward must be present, to answer to his or her name, and to be inspected by the master or matron.

XVIII. The boys and girls who are inmates of the workhouse shall, for three of the working hours at least every day, be respectively instructed in reading, writing, and in the principles of the Christian religion; and such other instructions shall be imparted to them as are calculated to train them to habits of usefulness, industry and virtue.

XIX. The diet of the paupers shall be so regulated as in no case to exceed, in quantity and quality of food, the ordinary diet of the able-bodied labourers living within the same district.

1 See page 96.

XXII. Any pauper may quit the workhouse, upon giving the master three hours' previous notice of his wish to do so; but no able-bodied pauper having a family shall so quit the house without taking the whole of such family with him or her, unless the board of guardians shall otherwise direct; nor shall any pauper, after so quitting the house, be again received into the house, unless in one of the modes prescribed in Rule I. for the admission of paupers.

XXVI. Any pauper, who shall neglect to observe such of the foregoing rules as are applicable to him or her;

Or who shall make any noise when silence is ordered;

Or use obscene or profane language;

Or by word or deed insult or revile any other pauper in the workhouse;

Or who shall not duly cleanse his or her person;

Or neglect or refuse to work;

Or pretend sickness;

Or disobey any of the legal orders of the master or matron, or other superintendent;

shall be deemed disorderly, and shall be placed in apartments provided for such offenders, or shall otherwise be distinguished in dress, and placed upon such diet as the board of guardians shall prescribe.

XXVII. Any pauper who shall, within seven days, repeat one of the offences specified in Rule XXVI;

Or who shall by word or deed insult or revile the master or matron, or any officer of the Union;

Or who shall be guilty of any act of drunkenness or indecency;

shall be deemed to be refractory, and shall be punished by such confinement and alteration of diet as the board of guardians shall direct, by any regulation for that purpose; but no pauper shall be confined under this rule for any misbehaviour or offence, for a longer period than 24 hours, or for such further space of time as may be necessary, in order to have such pauper carried before a justice of the peace, to be dealt with according to law.

On Saturday, the 25th of March, the long awaited day arrived when the doors of the Andover Workhouse were opened, and one hundred and eleven paupers whose age and

TABLE 'A'

	Hour of rising	Interval for Breakfast	Time for setting to work	Interval for Dinner	Time for leaving off work	Interval for supper	Time for going to bed
From 25th March to 29th September	6 o'clock	6.30 to 7	7 o'clock	12 to 1	6 o'clock	6 to 7	8
From 29th September to 25th March	7 o'clock	7.30 to 8	8 o'clock	12 to 1	6 o'clock	6 to 7	8

First Annual Report, p. 106.

sex is not recorded became the first of its inmates. There ought
to have been one hundred and twelve, but one by the name of
Robert Gill, for many years in receipt of the dole because of his
'most afflicted state', had seen the Workhouse looming ahead
and had chosen, in preference, to take his life. Many more
might have done so had they known of the trials and horrors
to come.

The Building Committee, naturally, were pleased. Hawley
wrote in a letter to Lefevre that he found the structure 'impos-
ing and commodious'. Best of all, the Guardians discovered,
casting up the annual accounts (the Poor Law year ending at
Lady Day), that the Workhouse System had produced already
a startling monetary benefit. Compared with the annual
average expenditure of the combined parishes before the
Union—£12,715—the past year's cost of relief had been only
£8,272. This was a saving—truly gratifying—of 35 per cent.[1]

The weekly meeting of the Board had finished before the
official hour for supper, before McDougal rang the bell, and
before, in total, decorous silence, the paupers assembled
separately, to eat it: 6 ounces of bread for the men, 5 ounces of
bread for the women; for each an ounce and a half of cheese;
the Guardians having prohibited beer, only icy water to drink.

At eight, all would have gone to bed, and at nine some
might have heard the porter, Uriah Ashford, lock the gates. If
any had dared to look out of the windows to watch the moonlit
road beneath they might, later, have spotted McDougal
limping away to the inns of Andover. Later still they might
have seen him lurching back, singing and swearing. For every
Saturday night he got drunk; and every Saturday night in his
cups he regaled his friends with boisterous songs and vowed,
between them, with military oaths, to murder every single
pauper in the Workhouse.

1 Fourth Annual Report, p. 63.
D

PART TWO

The Scandal

'That this act *must,* in effect, be repealed, we have no doubt; but at the same time, the fact that such a law did once exist in this Christian and civilized land will for centuries to come be a deep and damning stain both upon the Ministers that proposed and the Parliament that passed it.'

The Times. February 9th, 1835.

Chapter 6

THE EARLY YEARS of the reign of Victoria, 1837–1844, years of the worst economic depression that had ever afflicted the British people, were, for the Poor Law Commission at least, just because of the state of the country and the countless numbers of unemployed who were forced to enter the workhouses or starve, years of dramatic progress and fruitful achievement.

In these truly terrible years, when, due to financial collapse first in America and then at home, the nation's business came to a halt and more than a million paupers starved from simple lack of any employment, the greatest problem that faced the Commission was not so much its actual work of applying and spreading the Workhouse System, as keeping at bay its powerful enemies who were bent on its abolition. For, in the summer of 1839, five years after its formation, the Commission's term of office had to be renewed; and all those who had always opposed it—John Walter, their leading spokesman, a handful like him in the House of Commons, many ordinary, thinking citizens, and thousands of others since converted, some by reading *Oliver Twist*, others by what they had actually observed—determined by every means in their power to oppose its further continuance.[1]

---

1 Others had not been converted—like Lord Melbourne, the Prime Minister (who, as Home Secretary, had presided over the birth of the Commission). Speaking of *Oliver Twist* he said to Queen Victoria, 'It's all among Workhouses, and Coffin Makers, and Pickpockets, ... I don't *like* those things; I wish to avoid them; I don't like them in *reality*, and therefore I don't wish to see them represented' (quoted in *The Girlhood of Queen Victoria*; V.II., p. 144). If he, as head of the Government, felt like this, it is not surprising that his colleagues did not worry too much about people like John Walter.

John Walter's line of attack, common enough in the press today but less familiar in the 1830's, was quite simply to kill the Commission by sheer weight of propaganda. In every single edition of *The Times*, each day, every week, month after month, year by year, from the time that continuance became an issue in July, 1839, to July, 1842, when at last the idea was approved, a torrent of articles, letters and reports warned his readers what it would mean—not continuance but rather permanence, and urged them to rally against it.

Certainly, too, in these years, it had not been hard for John Walter, equipped as he was with dozens of reporters, nor indeed for anybody else provided only with eyes and ears, to learn that the work of the Poor Law Commission had not been quite so humane and perfect as alleged in the Annual Reports.

For, by the summer of 1842, every parish in England[1] and Wales had been forced to accept the Commission's authority, been made to unite with others locally, and compelled to subscribe to a common workhouse; and once the paupers had tried them out, and once a few had managed to escape, terrible tales had begun to be heard about what went on inside them.

A complete list of all the horrors exposed by Walter and many others would fill a book of a thousand pages; such a book as was actually compiled by G. R. Wythen Baxter entitled *The Book of the Bastiles* published in 1841, as part of the fight against continuance.

Because, as unemployment spread in the wake of increasing commercial collapse, and as more and more of the unemployed were forced by starvation to apply to the workhouses—far more than had ever been planned and far more than could ever be taken—the Poor Law Commissioners lost their grip; and harsher and harsher measures came to be adopted by the boards of guardians' masters and matrons to prevent their workhouses being engulfed by the hungry, inexorable tide.

In the name of the sacred workhouse principle that life within should be 'less eligible' than the lowest form of life without, every kind of crime was committed. The inmates' diet was frequently reduced; husbands and wives were kept apart, not only at night to prevent them cohabiting (and thus producing extra paupers) but also, illegally, during the daytime;

1 Except for a very few. See eighth Annual Report, p. 30.

children were torn away from their mothers and beaten brutally for daring to weep; and those children who were illegitimate, and those women who had painfully borne them, were kept apart, even from the others. The catalogue of tales like these is endless. The facts of one, from the workhouse at Eton, must serve as a text for the rest.

The Eton Workhouse,[1] like the one at Andover, had been built in the early days of the Poor Law—by the same architect on the same plan—and early on had come into the news for harsh treatment of mothers of bastards, one of whom, Ann Boddy, had refused to accept her badge of shame, a distinctive yellow workhouse gown, with nearly fatal consequences. At the same time, and perhaps because of it, the Board of Guardians had sacked the master, a retired artillery sergeant-major, on a charge of committing incest. After him had come another who had only survived for eighteen months before discharge for gross incompetence. The next master had been Joseph Howe, also a former sergeant-major, six and a half feet in height, aged forty, extremely muscular, who had held the post of master before in another workhouse up in the midlands. He came to Eton in 1840. With him, on 25th December, the disgusting story begins.

One of the paupers under his care was Elizabeth Wyse, a married woman, described by observers as 'weak and diminutive', whose child of only two-and-a-half had, in the course of bitter weather, contracted painful chilblains. She had, for a while, been allowed to sleep with it; for which act of grace and humanity she had, of course, got Howe's permission, having normally to remain elsewhere according to the usual workhouse rules. For some reason on Christmas Day, allegedly because the child was better, he had told her not to sleep with it any longer.

Instead, he had said she could visit it daily; but when he had found her two days later, bathing its feet and changing its bandages, he had told her to leave the nursery at once. When she refused he had lost his temper, dragged her violently down

1 The Assistant Commissioner in charge of its construction described it as, '. . . one of the most complete establishments of the kind in England. The perfect separation and means of classification of the sexes, and in short the arrangements altogether, surpass any establishment for the reception of paupers I have ever seen.' Including furniture, etc., it was to cost about £7,000; '. . . a splendid building.' P.R.O. M.H. 12/457.

the staircase, cast her into the workhouse cage, known to the inmates as the Black Hole, a narrow cell with a barred window which was unglazed and could not be closed except by a broken wooden shutter, and imprisoned her there in solitary confinement. He had left her thus for twenty-four hours with no coat, bedding, straw, food, water, or even a chamber pot. The night was the coldest for many years, the thermometer recording a frost of 20° F.

The following morning he had let her out, sent her up to the women's day room, given her a bowl of unpalatable gruel, the cold remains of the inmates' breakfast, and ordered her back to her cell to clean it as, naturally, without a utensil she had, inevitably, soiled the floor. This was a task she had found impossible, being literally frozen stiff. Howe, losing his temper again, had picked her up in his arms 'like a bird', carried her struggling back to the cell, and locked her up for a further seven hours.

Luckily for her, a few days afterwards, one of the ex-officio guardians, the Hon. and Rev. Godolphin Osborne, came to hear of Howe's brutality and lodged a complaint with the local magistrates. Howe was charged with common assault, found guilty and fined ten pounds.

Here the matter might have remained and Howe might easily have kept his post, since efficient masters were hard to find and in other respects he had worked satisfactorily; but as a result of widespread publicity, the entire case being covered by *The Times* as well, of course, as the local newspapers, another story came to light: that Howe had been in a scandal before, in his previous post in the workhouse at Brackley. Here, during the summer before, he had scalded a little boy to death, pouring over him a bucket of water which, he said, he had thought was cold but, in fact, had proved to be boiling. Only the fact that no one then (although afterwards they changed their minds) could believe that Howe could have acted on purpose had saved him from being sent to prison, had saved him even from being dismissed, had caused him, only after a hint, to offer his resignation.[1] He had, thus, brought to Eton a still technically

---

1 At Brackley, too, during the previous summer, the ratepayers of the union had presented a 'splendid silver tureen' costing £130 to the Chairman of the Board of Guardians, Colonel Cartwright, 'as a token of respect for his able services . . .'. *Northampton Mercury*, 6th June, 1840.

unblemished character. This disclosure, however, finished him. Brought before the Assistant Commissioner at the next meeting of the Board of Guardians, he received the treatment he thoroughly deserved, instant, ignoble dismissal.

As well as scandals such as this, exposed to the last unhappy detail and published in the anti-Poor Law press in every county in England and Wales, telling attacks were made on the Commission in novels, pamphlets and articles. Apart, of course, from *Oliver Twist*, the popularity of which was such that even the Poor Law Commissioners admitted (in an obvious reference to Dickens' masterpiece in a special report they prepared on continuance) that 'such a pathetic and saleable narrative' had influenced people widely against them, an extremely damaging article appeared in the Tory monthly, *Blackwood's Magazine*.

Published in April, 1838, immediately after the terrible winter in which the cost of relief had been high, it proposed as an extra measure of economy that the bodies of all who died in the workhouse be put to use in various ways to reduce the outlay of management. Instead of incurring an expensive burial—a parish coffin cost 8/6d—their skins should be flayed and tanned for leather, their bones be carved into spoons and forks,[1] and their flesh be made into nourishing soup for the loved ones left behind them.

Blackwood's then was widely read, and although the proposal was only a joke and was shrugged aside by the Poor Law Commissioners as merely another ridiculous example of the lengths to which their opponents would go, it became at once a workhouse spectre which no denial could ever erase. The amount of harm it did was enormous; and only its obviously fictional character, and only the respectability of *Blackwood's*, prevented many who hated the Poor Law from thinking that, at a later date, and if the Commission achieved continuance, it might, in fact, unknown to the public, really be put into practice.

A pamphlet even worse than this—worse because it was seriously meant—appeared towards the end of the year by the hand of an unknown 'Marcus'. Written, it was said, by one of the Commissioners, an imputation that was quite erroneous, it suggested solving the problem of the poor by limiting the

1 There was no cutlery in the workhouses in the early days. The inmates used their fingers.

number of their children. Comparing paupers to the slaves of old whose children often were strangled at birth, it proposed a family maximum of three, with infanticide for all the rest. As strangulation was rather brutal and out of tune with modern sentiment, it offered instead the agency of 'gaz'. What better use could be found for such a miraculous invention!

It adverted, last, to the kind of cemetery in which their tiny frames might rest.[1]

> . . . let there be a burial ground . . . call it rather a repository, for the privileged remains of these infants unadmitted into life. Let it have nothing funereal about it, but all that is cheerful and agreeable. Imagine then a colonnade, closed and gently warmed in winter, fresh in summer, verdant always, yet not expensive in exotics, not too distant for the daily disport of all classes, yet silencing vulgarity by an aimiable and religious formality. Let this be the infants' paradise; every parturient female will be considered as enlarging or embellishing it. This field of fancy will amuse her confinement, and will please by the reflection that her labour will have been not in vain, and that even posterity are to be the better for it.

Following closely after *Blackwood's*, 'Marcus's' pamphlet provoked a storm in every corner of the country. Questions were asked by Members of Parliament, outraged letters were published in the press, and Poor Law agitators up in the midlands where the Workhouse System had just been applied— in some places such as Todmorden in the face of such extensive riots that the workhouses never opened their doors—defied the danger of prosecution and publicly accused the Commissioners of having written it. The latter tried at first to be silent; but, in January, 1839, as a new cold spell developed even harsher than the year before; as the Thames froze throughout its length; as every workhouse was jammed to capacity and rations were even shorter than usual; they were forced finally to admit its existence, to repudiate utterly all its proposals, and also to issue a 'solemn denial' of knowledge or hand in its authorship.

1 'The BOOK OF MURDER! A vade-mecum for the Commissioners and Guardians of the NEW POOR LAW throughout Great Britain and Ireland, being an exact reprint of The Infamous Essay on the Possibility of Limiting Populousness by MARCUS, ONE OF THE THREE.'

In view of the fact that 1839 was the year in which the Commission lapsed unless renewed by Act of Parliament; and because of the scandals unearthed by *The Times*; of the troublesome effects of *Blackwood's* and 'Marcus'; also of petitions against continuance which, to the House of Commons alone, bore almost half a million signatures;[1] the Home Secretary asked the Commission to make a report on the popularity of the Poor Law.

Written in December, 1838, at the very height of the riots in the midlands and the revelation of the 'Marcus' proposals, it proved, luckily for those in authority, an extremely comforting document. Brushing aside the riots and petitions as nothing more than the work of agitators who were just as ready to speak for the Chartists as they were to petition against the corn laws, it pointed out that the recent troubles had taken place in three unions which had not yet been furnished with workhouses (in fact, they were protests against their adoption) of which, as a result, there was no experience nor, therefore, grounds for any complaint. In those unions which had got workhouses, now nearly six hundred, in almost every district in the country, conditions were peaceful and satisfactory. Calm would return, the report considered, as soon as the remaining districts were unionised and as soon as the Workhouse System was fully in force. As to the question of public opinion, that such calm already existed in all areas with efficient workhouses seemed to show that the law was approved since no Act could be enforced for long in the teeth of widespread democratic protest. In fact, extensive inquiry had proved that in every part the law was popular, not only amongst the labouring poor who were reaping the benefits of industry and thrift but also, of course, amongst the ratepayers who (apart from saving money) had come to value the Poor Law Commission as a useful, impartial, knowledgeable agency. The report closed by quoting the opinions of various Assistant Commissioners. All of them came to the same conclusion: that on the whole the System worked; that by and large it operated well; that taken generally it was not unpopular. One of them thought that if it were repealed its absence would lead to dangerous riots. Of the Andover area, a'Court wrote:

---

1 House of Commons, Reports of Select Committees on Public Petitions.

> Notwithstanding the conscientious scruples of some very estimable men, the determined opposition of others, and the very natural dissatisfaction of many interested parties, the pubic opinion in my purely agricultural district is decidedly favourable both to the principle of the New Poor Law and to the mode of its administration.[1]

Armed with such a consoling assurance, written certainly by the very authority which most of all desired its acceptance, but all the same, presented sincerely, the Home Secretary, Lord John Russell, ought in the ordinary course of events to have found it easy to carry a Bill for the continuation of the Poor Law Commission without particular difficulty. Lord Melbourne's Government, however, were not then in a strong position; and, in fact, later on, faced with financial problems at home and a constitutional crisis in Jamaica, in the House of Commons they were actually defeated. The Queen's refusal to change her ladies-in-waiting, the so-called 'Bedchamber crisis', kept them in power until 1841; but during their final years in office they were forced to govern from day to day. As any plan to continue the Commission was bound to be fought with fanatical energy, the Home Secretary decided to postpone it; and, by means of a simple Act, did so twice, until 1841. Then Lord Melbourne's party fell. The Tories, pressed by greater problems—budget deficiencies, stagnation in trade, lack of employment and widespread hunger—decided, too, that they must defer it. So, from the summer of 1839 to the spring of 1842, much to the glee of all its opponents who saw in every day of delay a brighter prospect of final success, the Poor Law Commission merely survived in a state of uneasy abeyance.

For a brief moment the Commission's opponents basked in the hope of an imminent triumph because in the current general election many candidates had actually won—John Walter, in fact among them[2]—due to a promise to oppose the

1 Report on Public Opinion. P.R.O. H.O. 73/54. Dated 28th December, 1838.
2 At Nottingham, the first Tory to win the seat for thirty years. He was unseated on petition, however; due, he considered, to the animosity of Peel and Graham, though technically on the ground that his agent had used bribes. He did not enter Parliament again. (*History of The Times*, Vol II, pp. 6 and 540.)

Poor Law, and because, with a party now in office which had long deplored the Workhouse System, they thought they were bound to achieve its extinction. The result in the end was the other way about. For the new Tory Home Secretary was none other than Sir James Graham, not only once a prominent Whig but also a member of the Cabinet Committee which, in 1834, had actually drafted the Bill for the Poor Law; and he shared the view of Sir Robert Peel, the Prime Minister who followed Melbourne, that the only realistic course to adopt—as indeed was certainly the case—was to give the Commission a further mandate.

Thus, when the Bill to continue the Commission—in all, now, the fourth to be presented—finally came to be debated in Parliament, far from its hope of success being limited, its chance of failure was practically nil; since all the Whigs whose creation it was were bound, naturally, to continue to support it, and most of the Tories did so too, many in spite of election promises to do exactly the reverse. For whenever Graham expounded the facts which he did with knowledge, force and lucidity, he presented a case that was very convincing.

Whatever the faults of the Poor Law Commission, and no one, he said, pretended it was perfect, whatever the failings of any Commissioner, whatever the defects of any workhouse, or of any guardians, masters or matrons, two facts could not be disputed. First, that the poor were better cared for—and here he produced a mass of statistics—than in any other country in the world; second, the cost, high though it was—and here again he supplied the evidence—was far less than it had been earlier before the days of the Poor Law Commission, and quite certainly infinitely less than it would be supposing the Commission were dissolved and its work restored to the parish authorities. Of course abuses were bound to crop up in a vast agency such as the Commission, and of course, like everyone else he deplored them; but here again, compared to the past when abuses were hardly ever discovered and redress for the victims was almost impossible, the Poor Law Commission was a great improvement. The very fact that the press exposed them and usually obtained the culprit's dismissal proved how extremely well the System worked.

He closed his final speech as follows:

Deterred, then, by no improper fear—disregarding all personal obloquy that may attach to me on account of my enforcing what may be thought severe, but which, I believe firmly, will, in the long run, prove humane and salutary,— I cannot hesitate as to the course which I ought to adopt; and I earnestly entreat the House to pass the Bill with such a majority as will mark how united we are (without reference to party distinctions) on the propriety of continuing a measure so important to the interests of the poor and of the community at large.[1]

The Bill was passed by a large majority, renewing the Commission until 1847. The Commissioners must have sighed with relief; while in every workhouse in England and Wales which now commanded every locality like a chain of oppressive military outposts, every petty union official whose job had hung for so long in the balance must, frankly, have greeted the news with cheers.

1 *Hansard*, 22nd July, 1842.

Chapter 7

IN THE FIRST year of this period which came to a close with the Bill for continuance, the year 1837, the first in the reign of Queen Victoria and the first in the life of the Andover Workhouse, the petty officials chosen to run it, Christopher Dodson, the Chairman of the Board, his thirty-six fellow Guardians, and Mr. and Mrs. Colin McDougal, right from the start began their work in the way that they meant to go on.

First of all, as soon as possible, and long before they ought to have done so, they applied the screw that was feared the most, the dreaded Prohibitory Order. This Order enforced the rule that all relief at home should be stopped for all paupers who were able-bodied, the basic rule, in fact, of the Poor Law but one which, in most areas, to give the paupers time to adjust, had not been applied immediately. In Andover the Guardians enforced it at once because, in the view of William Hawley, the Assistant Commissioner then in charge, all was quiet within the Union; in fact, 'in a state of perfect tranquillity'; the Workhouse, also, completely ready, indeed 'perfected in every department'; so, as he wrote in a cheerful report, '. . . though the prohibitory rule has not yet been issued the Guardians are, notwithstanding, of their own accord carrying its provisions fully into effect'.[1] They did so, rigidly, throughout the winter, even throughout the famous freeze during three weeks of arctic weather with sixteen degrees of frost when, as Hawley himself admitted, many unions had flouted the law and permitted relief to be given in the home. He reported in March, 1838:

> The Unions to which the Rule has not been applied experienced considerable pressure during the continuance

1 P.R.O. M.H. 32/39. 1st January, 1838.

of the severe weather at the beginning of the Quarter which was yielded to in a greater or less degree by the majority, but in the Alton and Andover Unions it was successfully resisted.[1]

As a result, the paupers starved and, but for the kindness of local inhabitants who raised a subscription of £200 which they spent on food, coal and blankets, many, surely, would have starved to death. In the Workhouse, too, there was near starvation; and in December, Hugh Mundy, an elected Guardian for the parish of Andover, a true friend and champion of the poor—almost the only one they had—requested the Board to ask the Commissioners to allow the inmates a Christmas Dinner. He received a reply on the 23rd:

> The Poor Law Commissioners for England and Wales regret that they do not feel justified in assenting to the proposition contained in your letter of the 18th instant that, the paupers in the Union Workhouse should be regaled on the ensuing Christmas day with a good Dinner & Beer, to be provided at the expense of the Guardians & others willing to contribute by voluntary subscriptions.
>
> The Commissioners consider that this proposition is directly at variance with the principles upon which the efficacy of the Workhouse System depends (namely) that the condition of the pauper inmate of the Workhouse should not be desired or envied by the independent person; and the Comm[rs] therefore cannot consent that the inmates of the Workhouse should be supplied with indulgencies which too many of those who support themselves without parochial aid are obliged altogether to forgo.[2]

The Guardians met the same day, and Christopher Dodson wrote to Hawley:

> We are, I think, going on pretty well—we disposed of all the cases this morning in one half hour—our numbers in the Workhouse have decreased since we saw you, they are today 148.

1 P.R.O. M.H. 32/39. 31st March, 1838.
2 P.R.O. M.H. 12/10661. 22nd December, 1837.

Mrs Dodson unites in the best wishes of the season to you with my dear Hawley

Yrs always truly
Ch[r] Dodson.[1]

So the year 1837, at least for the paupers inside the Workhouse, came to a hungry close.

Another form of persecution, begun as soon as the Workhouse was opened and carried on for many years, was directed against unmarried mothers. To conceive an illegitimate child, as well as being a sinful act was felt, too, to be an outrage (only, of course, in the case of paupers who had to apply to the parish for support) because of the extra burden on the rates; and for this reason all the authorities, both of the church as well as the state, did all they could to prevent it happening, and to punish those who defied their efforts.

In the Andover Union, as elsewhere, there were many children who were 'base born', to use the customary cruel expression, so that once the Guardians had settled down and set in motion the Prohibitory Order, they turned their attention to 'unchaste women'. The Minutes record their moment of decision:

It having been suggested to the Guardians that the most beneficial results have been experienced in other unions from placing a distinguishing Badge on Singlewomen in the workhouse having a Bastard Child or Children, Resolved that such a Badge be obtained forthwith and in future adopted in this Union.

The badge they chose was a yellow stripe, sewn across the grey gown which had to be worn by all the inmates. Hawley reported two months later in a long letter addressed to the Commissioners that the move had proved a great success and that several women had left the Workhouse as soon as the stripe had been forced upon them.

In the Alresford, Andover, Portsea Island and Westhampnett Unions a badge of distinction has been placed

1 P.R.O. M.H. 12/10661. 23rd December, 1837.

on women of immoral character with Bastard children with considerable effect, several having left the Houses in consequence, and the behaviour of the remainder having been much improved by the prospect of its removal on any moral amendment discovering itself.[1]

Later on, this practice was forbidden, but at least in the Workhouse at Andover—doubtless in many others also—other similar punishments remained. Mothers, suffering the pangs of labour, were not permitted medical attention except in cases of dangerous emergency; and, once the ordeal was past, whether the baby lived or not, they had to put up with an inquisition with many sharp and frightening rebukes from the Workhouse Chaplain, appointed by the Board.

At Andover, the Rev. Henry Manning Richards used to read from the *Priest's Companion*.

I must put you in mind that your salvation depends upon the truth of your repentance. Now, forasmuch as you became a sinner by breaking the laws of God, you have no ways of being restored to God's favour but by seeing the number and greatness of your sins, that you may hate them heartily, lament them sorely, and cry mightily to God for pardon. I will therefore set before you the laws of God, by which God will judge you, and I will ask you such questions as may be proper to call your sins to your remembrance; . . .

Your duty to God, you know, is to fear him, to love him, to trust in him, to honour and to obey him. Consider, therefore, seriously, have you lived as if there were no God to call you to an account?

Your duty to your neighbour is to love him as yourself. Have you so loved all men, as to wish and pray sincerely for their welfare?

Have you hated your enemies?

Have you paid due reverence in heart, in word, in behaviour, to your parents, and to all such as were over you in place and authority?

Have you been subject to sinful unadvised anger?

1 P.R.O. M.H. 32/39. 1st January, 1838.

Have you ever done anything to shorten the life of your neighbour?

Have you lived in malice or envy, or wished any man's death?

Have you been accustomed to sow strife and dissension amongst your neighbours?

Have you fallen into the sins of drunkenness, gluttony, tippling, or an idle life?

Have you kept yourself free from the sins of whoredom, impurity, or uncleanness?

Have you been subject to the evil habits of lying, slandering, or talebearing?

Have you ever given false evidence, out-faced the truth, or countenanced an evil cause?

Have you been pleased with evil reports, and have you been too forward to propagate them?

Have you been dissatisfied with the condition which God allotted to you?

Have you coveted your neighbour's goods, envied his prosperity, or been pleased with his misfortunes?

Have you done to others as you wish they should have done to you?

Can you call to mind any injury or injustice for which you ought to ask pardon, or make restitution?

And remember, you are told the truth, that the unrighteous and unjust shall not enter the kingdom of Heaven.

Is there anybody that has grievously wronged you, to whom you ought to be reconciled?

Remember that if you forgive not, you will not be forgiven; and that he will receive judgement without mercy, who hath showed no mercy.

Are you therefore in charity with all the world?

And now I will leave you for a while to God and to your own conscience, beseeching him to discover to you the charge that is against you, that you may know and confess, and bewail and abhor the errors of your life past, that your sins may be done away by his mercy, and your pardon sealed in Heaven before you go hence and be no more seen.

Whatever the mothers may have replied as they lay feebly listening to Richards, only partially quoted here as the full text is extremely long,[1] it is hard to believe that they felt shamed or any emotion except despair. Richards, then, was very young; perhaps time softened his approach as he married the vicar of Andover's daughter and was blessed himself with several children. In the early days of the Union, however, he must have frightened many of the inmates. Yet, no matter what he said or anyone else connected with the Workhouse, year after year the sin was committed; and single girls within the Union as well as others passing by were forced, like the mother of Oliver Twist, to ring the Workhouse bell in their hour of need.[2]

Another minor Workhouse official who started out as he meant to go on was Robert Cooke, of Weyhill,[3] Relieving Officer for a large district which included the town of Andover. His work was somewhat like a doctor's.[4] The poor in need came to his house (or he to them, if they were sick); he brought their cases before the Board; he then transmitted the Board's instructions—either so much relief per week, or, more often, an order to the Workhouse.

As no relief could be granted at all (except in the case of urgent necessity) without a Relieving Officer's order, every pauper knew and feared him. Christopher Dodson knew him too, not only because he saw him at the Workhouse but also because they were neighbours in the country. Thus between Dodson and the poor, Cooke's position as an intermediary was, from the start, a strong one.

As Cooke's home at Weyhill (he had just built himself a new house) was four miles to the west of Andover; and as Andover had more inhabitants and therefore inevitably more paupers than any other place in his district, the elected Guardians of

1 S.C.A.U., p. 1,417.
2 'The surgeon leaned over the body, and raised the left hand. "The old story," he said, shaking his head: "no wedding-ring, I see. Ah! Good night!" ' *Oliver Twist*, Ch. 1. The workhouse described by Dickens was not at Andover. It is thought most likely to have been at Chatham.
3 See Ch. 4, p. 60. Cooke (spelt without an 'e' in the parish records) had been overseer of the poor and collector of the rates at Weyhill since 1821; and his father before him.
4 See Ch. 5, p. 75 for the Poor Law Commission's official instructions to Relieving Officers; see also Appendix B below.

Andover parish first of all opposed his appointment, and then, being outvoted at the Board, proposed that at least he should live in the town.

Cooke, however, refused to do so, and since he enjoyed the confidence of Dodson and thus, in effect, the support of the Board which always did what the latter suggested he was able to win a second victory when the Andover Guardians proposed formally that his case be put to the Poor Law Commission.

The Minutes record his opponents' defeat:

Proposed by Mr. Goodall and seconded by Mr. Langstaff That Mr. Cooke the Relieving Officer for District No. 1. be required to reside in Andover and that a Memorial to that effect be forwarded to the Poor Law Commissioners.

Amendment proposed by Major Gardiner and seconded by Mr. Thomas Dowling That no such Memorial be presented which on being put to the meeting was carried by a large majority.

2nd May, 1836.

Not to be beaten, Goodall and Langstaff then, on behalf of the Andover Vestry, wrote to the Poor Law Commissioners direct. Doubtless thanks to the advice of Hawley who came to Andover shortly afterwards and must have heard of the move from Dodson, the Commissioners decided not to be caught, and only replied by writing to the Board, declining to interfere.

So Cooke was able to stay where he was, four miles away from Andover; and any pauper who wished to see him on a Sunday, Tuesday, Wednesday or Friday, the days when he visited other parishes, had four miles to walk to his house. Then, whatever relief was given, a loaf of bread or a ticket of admission, had, of course, to be taken away, the same distance back to the cottage or four miles to the gates of the Workhouse. Eight miles was too far for many paupers to attempt to walk and numbers died without ever seeing him. Others set out and never came back; finding relief at last in death as they paused for a moment under a hedge, or in the darkness lost their way and tumbled into a ditch or fell into a snowdrift.

Once the paupers were in the Workhouse the question arose of what to do with them; and having taken Hawley's advice that every inmate ought to work, no matter what his age or condition—a view that was shared by the Poor Law Commissioners—the Guardians decided to solve the problem by installing equipment for pounding bones, the dust of which was used for manure.

The apparatus required for this, recommended by the Poor Law Commission, was a long iron bar or rammer, weighing twenty to thirty pounds, the end of which was split into points, and an iron-bound wooden box, a little over a foot in depth and one-and-a-half feet across, the sides of which could be lifted off to enable the dust to be taken out, the bottom of which, made of iron, was fixed firmly to the floor. [Plate 13]

On this subject, Hawley had written:[1]

> The fact of confinement in a workhouse being voluntary and not compulsory (inasmuch as the admittance of a pauper is conditional upon that alternative) must not be lost sight of, and as a proof that it neither tends to create ennui or despondency, but on the contrary that it stimulates men to exertion who would otherwise be listlessly dozing their time away in idleness, or consuming it in immoral pursuits—the aged and infirm paupers (who are usually considered past work) in the Westhampnett workhouse are employed many of them spontaneously at the Bone Mill for several hours during the day, and the profit derived to the union from the labour of these volunteers generally amounts to about two shillings per day per head.

Whatever the paupers did in Sussex, the county in which Westhampnett lay, however much they enjoyed their work, less could be said about those in Hampshire, especially those in the Andover Union, a number of whom, after a trial, decided that 'dozing away their time', even if they starved to do it, was altogether preferable.

Hawley, forgetting his earlier report, noted the fact with evident triumph.

> The work now carrying on in the several workhouses by the male paupers consists in grinding corn and Bones . . . in one week after a Mill had been provided in the Andover

1 P.R.O. M.H. 32/39. 9th September, 1837.

Union, 8 able bodied paupers who with their families amounting to 43 individuals had been a considerable time in the workhouse, left it on account of the undesirable nature of the employment.[1]

Many paupers testified later as to its 'undesirability'. The smell, alone, was indescribable, making many of them very ill; fragments of bone flew in their faces, scarring numbers of them quite severely; and the plain effort of lifting the crusher for eight hours every day until they had pounded a hundredweight of bones, the usual quantity given by McDougal, literally almost broke their backs. Even their children were forced to do it, little boys of nine or ten, who had to work together in pairs, holding a single crusher between them, climbing up on the edges of the box to obtain the necessary lift for the downward stroke. Their arms cracked, their hands bled; their sobs were choked by the terrible stench, their tears were turned to mud by dust that clogged their bloodshot eyes.

As the first year came to a close in the summer of 1838 when, as it happened, Hawley departed, the Guardians, taking stock of their work, must have considered it with satisfaction. Apart from making substantial economies (officially 28 per cent of the cost of relief before the Union and before the paupers had come into the Workhouse) they had got the labourers where they wanted them, in a state of hungry acquiescence far removed from the dangerous mood so lately shown in the Labourers' Revolt; and had found in Colin McDougal and his wife a pair whose military life and training had made them exactly right for the job. Nothing now remained to be done except, it seemed, to continue the work in the manner so well begun.

In the early days of the New Poor Law, to inspect the workhouse was a charitable duty, and a book was kept in the porter's lodge in which the visitors could note their findings. In this first year of its life, not one single observer, doctors, parsons, gentry or their wives, had anything but praise for what they saw.

I have received the most perfect satisfaction and gratification from an inspection of the arrangements of the

1 P.R.O. M.H. 32/39. 1st January, 1838.

establishment in every respect [wrote Mrs. E. M. James]; but my crowning satisfaction is derived from my conversation with Mr. McDougal, the soundness, liberality, and singular good sense of his views, which I have rarely met with, even in individuals in association of many committees of persons whose single and sincere views have been the good of the poor. I depart with a most pleasant impression of the whole, and great esteem for the master and mistress's zeal and fitness for the Christian work in which they are engaged.

Dr. L. T. Nayle observed:

I consider this house for industry, cleanliness, and good order, both internally and externally, cannot be exceeded, with the healthy appearance of men, women, and children, and does great credit to the governor, etc., and a pattern to other houses, and shows the sound sense in having a military man to control the establishment, and everything open to inspection by Mrs. McDougal, with great civility.[1]

Only the two Misses Etwall, whose brother was Andover's Member of Parliament, glimpsed behind the military veil and saw that the inmates were thin and hungry. They, too, praised the arrangement, but thought that there ought to be extra bread, especially to go with the bacon.

On this subject, the Guardians demurred, and once again, supported by Hawley, his last advice before his departure, they firmly resisted all suggestions that extra bread or beer should be given, even to those who were pounding bones or even, for once, to all the inmates to celebrate the Coronation.

In the market square in the centre of Andover a feast was spread for the latter event at which the poor who were not in the Workhouse were regaled with traditional English fare— roast beef and plum puddings—with beer for the men and tea for the women. Then, for more than a thousand children there were games and dancing on the Common Acre in order, in the words of the Mayor, Mr. Heath, 'to stamp on the minds of the

1 S.C.A.U., p. 1,388.

young and rising generation a lasting impression of being coeval with our youthful, virtuous, and beloved Queen Victoria'.

Thus Hawley took his leave, with a last report to the Poor Law Commissioners in which he deplored the 'excess of loyalty' which had caused the guardians of certain workhouses, not, happily, those at Andover, to give their paupers Coronation rations. He was posted up to a northern district in which, safely away from his wife, he forgot his views on 'unchaste women', the Badge of Shame and the yellow stripe, and took a mistress, Margaret Graham. His legal marriage had proved to be barren, but Margaret Graham gave him a 'base born' child.[1]

---

1 He died in 1874, aged eighty, still in the service of the Poor Law Board (the successor of the Poor Law Commission) as a Poor Law Inspector, thus serving the organisation for forty years. He left £200 p.a. to 'William Hawley (my natural son by Margaret Graham, otherwise Hawley, now residing at Rockcliffe, near Carlisle).'

Chapter 8

In the years that followed Hawley's departure, 1839–1845, the terrible years of the 'hungry forties', nothing happened in the Andover Workhouse to break the established rhythm of life—the daily penance endured by the inmates, the weekly meetings of the Board of Guardians, the quarterly inspections of Hawley's successors, the annual election of Union officials—so that, as the time went quietly by with Colin McDougal still the Governor and Christopher Dodson still the Chairman, the meetings of the Board grew shorter and shorter in spite of the rising number of inmates. Habit made the Guardians brisk, and hunger made the paupers submissive. The fears aroused by the Labourers' Revolt at long, long last began to subside.

The success of affairs in the Andover Union was due, more than anything else, to the personal activity of Christopher Dodson. Born in 1793 and thus aged forty-two when first appointed Chairman of the Board, he came of a long line of clergymen stretching back to the 17th century, of whom his grandfather and father successively had been the Rectors of Hurstpierpoint in Sussex for ninety-four years. He, too, was to live long and perform his sacred duties diligently. Rector of Grately and Penton Mewsey, both parishes in the Andover Union, to the former of which (next to Amport, so much disturbed in the Labourers' Revolt) he came at the age of twenty-six, he retained both until he died at the handsome age of eighty-three. As it proved, he was destined also to serve as Chairman of the Board of Guardians for almost half his life.

Dodson's admirable sense of duty was marred by the manner in which he performed it. Sharing the useful beliefs of his time that the social order was arranged by God; that protests against it, therefore, were sinful; that charity, naturally, became the rich; that humility, equally, became the poor; and that, of all the many sins that the poor continually seemed to commit, by far the worst was that of sloth; he treated the paupers extremely severely. He had, too, a sarcastic address which silenced not only the wretched inmates on the very, very rare occasions when they found themselves before him at the Board, but also nearly all the Guardians, most of whom, as yeomen or trades-men, felt themselves to be socially below him and were used already to following his wishes. Also, he trusted Colin McDougal, mainly because the latter stood up to him (who, as a former sergeant-major was not, of course, afraid of anybody), approved of his being a disciplinarian, and often used, jokingly, to say that a dose or two of 'Mac's medicine'—a week or two inside the Workhouse—was the finest cure he knew for anything. Bent on sternly doing his duty, he forgot how harsh, for a country parson, his attitude seemed to be.

All who paid the rates, however; all, that is, but the very few who had always opposed the Workhouse System, con-sidered Dodson's method excellent. When, by 1839, the cost of a loaf had actually doubled from what it had been in 1835, and when, thanks to Dodson's efficiency, the cost per head of feeding the inmates had, amazingly, stayed the same, they decided to mark their profound esteem by making him a presentation.

Eight days before Christmas, fifty of Dodson's warmest admirers gave him a banquet at the Star Inn and, with all the usual speeches, handed him a splendid service of plate of four massive covered dishes, the lids of which were elegantly chased, and a beautiful epergne with four branches. It bore the following simple inscription:

Presented to the Rev. C. Dodson, M.A. in testimony of his able and zealous services as Chairman of the Andover Board of Guardians, under the New Poor Law. A.D. 1839.

Its cost, also, was a warming testament, £270; enough, on the Andover scale of subsistance, to keep a normal, healthy pauper alive for five years.

Dodson's only admitted failure, freely declared when he took the Chairmanship, was an inability to read accounts; and later on, in 1842, it gave his victims inside the Workhouse the only cause they ever had for amusement. In that spring, John Maude, the son of a former Mayor of Andover, the collector of the rates for Andover parish, and managing clerk to the Clerk to the Guardians, suddenly vanished with £2,000. He was run to earth a year later by Henry Barefoot, a London policeman, and brought in handcuffs back to Andover. Dodson, of course, was highly delighted, and planned to put him in prison for years. But Maude's attornies, Cockburn and Saunders, found a flaw in the bill against him, and on a legal technicality actually managed to get him off. Dodson's rage can only be imagined. While, of course, he was not to blame since the Union accounts had all been audited and all, invariably, found correct, for the first time in nine yers he had to face, from some of his colleagues, a discreet amount of criticism.

The other person whose sense of duty caused the System to work so well was, of course, the Governor, Colin McDougal. Born in 1793 (the same year as Christopher Dodson) in a small village close to Perth and taught as a child the trade of weaver, he joined the artillery in 1807, fought at the battle of Waterloo, was given a discharge as 'worn out' as a staff sergeant in 1836, his character being described as 'exemplary'. When on duty in the north of France, his horse had fallen and crushed his leg which had given him trouble ever since, swelling painfully whenever he was tired. The accident, too, had affected his chest in which, at times, he had agonising spasms. Apart from this and indigestion caused, no doubt, by army food, to which he had been a martyr for years and which made him, sometimes, extremely irritable, his health and physique were extremely good. Of medium height with a fair complexion, blue eyes and brown hair; with, of course, a Highland accent and a calm, determined, respectful manner, he was, when he first arrived in Andover, still a man with plenty of character and vigour.

Naturally enough when he first arrived he thought he was meant to look after the inmates, to help them understand the System which, of course, was entirely new; to see they behaved according to the rules; to distribute their meagre rations fairly; and generally, as far as he possibly could, to keep them passive, healthy and content. Quite soon Dodson's attitude: his institution of the Badge of Shame; his application of the Prohibitory Order; his refusal to sanction a Christmas Dinner; and all his other acts of tyranny, made him realise he had made a mistake. Instead, he began to bully the inmates and to make their lives in the Workhouse miserable. Of course, they left whenever they could; as time went by, with increasing frequency. Dodson praised his powers of command, and his common sense and loyalty.

Another duty sternly performed to the satisfaction of the Chairman of the Board was the education of the children. As every child who was raised in the Workhouse (most of whom were illegitimate) was expected to leave and earn its living as soon as it reached the age of puberty; and as, of course, whatever it did—the girls in service, boys in apprenticeship—strict obedience was always paramount; discipline was taught at an early age.

No child was too small, in the view of Mr. and Mrs. McDougal, to receive an occasional flick of the cane, so that long before they did any lessons, the girls being taught by Elizabeth McDougal, the boys being taught by her brother Joseph, both of whom were in their teens and both of whom were as strict as their parents, they learnt the meaning of the verb 'to whip'. When they were older they ran away, and when they were caught they were flogged severely, many cases being noted in the Minutes. Recorded, too, in 1841 was the tale of little Jimmy Brown whose age was only three and a half, who kept on making a mess in his bed as the Workhouse food had 'relaxed his bowels' and his mother's absence had naturally upset him. One Sunday McDougal thrashed him, chasing after him round the cot, down the stairs and into the dining room to which, in terror, Jimmy fled. By then, McDougal was in a rage which was not improved by the state of his nerves which were always bad on Sunday mornings, due to drink on Saturday night. When at last he caught the child who was only dressed in a thin chemise, he beat his bottom with all his might and finally broke the cane across his back. The next day with the help of a clergyman his father sued McDougal for assault. Although the Guardians paid for the defence and deposed that McDougal, 'tender and fatherly', had never been known to maltreat the children, he was found guilty, fined a shilling, and charged the costs of half a guinea or, in lieu, a fortnight's imprisonment. Dodson considered this most unfair, and reported the case to the Poor Law Commissioners in the hope that the costs could be charged to the rates. Receiving, however, a negative reply he gave McDougal the money himself. Luckily the child and its parents left which relieved the Union of having further to support them.

Another of the paupers driven away by McDougal's sense of duty to the Chairman was a girl called Hannah Joyce. In March, 1845, she came into the Workhouse with a little child, aged about five weeks, which died suddenly in bed in her arms three nights after her arrival. Two of the other women in the ward rang the bell for Mrs. McDougal who, with abuse, refused to come (having, as it happened, a painful leg) and threatened, unless they went back to bed, to drench them both with a bucket of water. After a while they rang again, and one went down to explain what had happened. Mrs. McDougal then came up not, of course, in the best of moods; and because the child was illegitimate, and because Hannah, the year before, had lost another base born baby in rather similar and sudden circumstances, Mrs McDougal addressed her roughly, called her a 'good for nothing brute', and said that now she would hang for murder. McDougal, following, rather drunk, added, 'Yes, and you'll go to Hell. You're nothing better than a whore and a faggot.' Hannah, already very upset, was now convulsed with fright as well as sorrow. Perhaps because she was making a noise or possibly just as a further punishment she was ordered then to go downstairs to spend the rest of the night in the mortuary beside the corpse of her infant. When she flatly refused to do so she was taken away by a mad nurse who was known as 'The Devil' to all the inmates because of her brutal behaviour in the wards, and locked inside an empty dormitory. A post mortem the following day showed that the child had died of bronchitis. In spite of this, as an extra penalty, entirely contrary to normal practice, McDougal made her collect the corpse, then secured in a tiny coffin, and carry it herself through the streets of Andover three quarters of a mile to the parish graveyard. Because the child had not been baptised it could not be given a Christian burial. Instead, it was registered as 'stillborn', left on the floor inside the church, and later on, without a stone, swiftly interred by the sexton. Hannah by now had suffered enough and prepared to leave as soon as she might, according to the rule, the ensuing Saturday, the day on which the Guardians met. McDougal still had a treat in store for her. When she departed he drummed her out, ordering most of the female inmates to give her what was known as a 'skimmington', a noisy, degrading, public parade, making her pass between their ranks as they waited for her outside the Workhouse banging their plates and mugs with stones. At that time the Guardians were meeting, and McDougal was with them beside the Chairman. When it began he explained the noise and immediately went outside to stop it. Dodson actually broke into a laugh though he did say, a moment later, that he thought that 'Mac' was exceeding his duty. Hannah, weeping, trudged homewards, seven miles to her parish of Chilbolton. A Mrs. Grace, one of the inmates and one of McDougal's trusted minions with whom he had secretly had an affair, was sent on a mission that was hardly necessary, to ensure that she actually left the town. McDougal, grinning, watched them go; sent the demonstrators back indoors; and then returned to his place inside the Board Room.

McDougal's activities with Mrs. Grace had led to a row of horrific proportions from which, in the end, he derived a substantial benefit. Following supper one Saturday night, a time at which he was always drunk and not at all in a mood to be crossed, his wife had questioned him about a rumour that, on Sundays, when she went to church, he and Grace, who was then the cook, would meet and embrace one another in the kitchen. After a burst of denial and abuse, he had staggered to his feet and hit her. Later on, as the fight developed, two of his daughters had woken up and run to two of the inmates for help. By then it was after twelve o'clock and coming back they had found McDougal, blood pouring from a wound in his head which his wife had managed to inflict with a cup, damning and blasting her eyes from a corner of the sofa. Getting up, he had roared for his gun, but after a step collapsed on the floor. Mrs. McDougal was sitting also, with blood all over her face and bosom. One of the inmates, fetched by the children, afterwards told the rest of the story.

> Mr. McDougal laid there; his head was bleeding too, and there was blood on the carpet and on the wainscot too. He kept swearing in an awful state; I never saw anybody look so dreadful in my life; he only kept swearing; he did not address anything to his wife; he said 'bloody' sometimes. Mrs. McDougal came out of the little sitting-room; she had got her dress off then, and pointing to her bosom, she said, 'Here I am, bloody Mary, the old name'. When I left the

room I left him there down on the floor. Mrs. McDougal
came out of the room, locked the door, and went to sleep
with her children, Jane Emma and Fanny. She locked
Mr. McDougal in the room. We got to bed again about
20 minutes past two o'clock on Sunday morning.[1]

The next day, the witness related, instead of going trustingly
to church, Mrs. McDougal sent for a rope and said she was going
to hang herself.

McDougal, however, was not abashed, and quite soon, to his
great delight, he discovered that most of the female inmates,
especially those who were young and maidenly, had been so
alarmed at his wife's behaviour, her violent passion and
threatened suicide, that his lusty advances were never reported.
'Come here, come here!' he used to command with a coaxing
smile when he wished to catch a girl and kiss her, softening his
broad Highland accent in a way that the inmates used to
mimic. Instead of running at once to his wife, they only
simpered, giggled and scuttled away.

One, Caroline Holt, recorded:

In what they call the girl's day-hall, something particular
occurred since Christmas. I then had the care of the
children; the children were in the school and it was in the
morning; he came in the first place to do something to the
window; he asked me to come and hold the window; I did
that, and he put his hand into my bosom; he said, 'How
beautiful and soft!' I said to Mr. McDougal, 'For God's sake,
take out your hand; if mistress was to see us, she would
think me to blame, and perhaps would kill me.' He went
away then. These liberties I have spoken of in the office
have taken place a great many times. I did not even then tell
Mrs. McDougal how Mr. McDougal treated me; I should not
have been believed; the weakest would have been sure to
have gone to the wall. I have no spite against Mr. and Mrs.
McDougal. I have been treated with kindness in this house,
and very great unkindness.[2]

1 S.C.A.U., p. 1,485.
2 S.C.A.U., p. 1,479.
E

Some of the older women submitted, having nothing to lose, amongst whom was Elizabeth Hutchins, a matron of more than average spirit who had passed an unusually interesting life, the details of which are worth recording. Born in 1793, the same year as Dodson and McDougal, in a cottage still inhabited today in the beautiful parish of Abbott's Ann, she had known hunger, literally from birth, her parents, Joseph and Elizabeth Brown, being even then supported by the parish. She had married in May, 1811, her husband being a deserted soldier who was taken back to his regiment and flogged only a fortnight after their wedding. Then she was forcibly taken to Chute, her husband's parish to the west of Andover which, by law, was compelled to support her because, clearly, she was still a pauper. Here she took up with a man called Winter with whom she lived for five years and to whom she bore a son called William. When she was found to be living with another when her husband (whose name was Charles Hutchins) returned at last from active service, she was taken down to Andover market, tied to a rope like a troublesome heifer, and sold to Winter for two-and-sixpence, an event of sufficient rustic charm to be given a report in the *Salisbury Journal*.[1] She lived with Winter for a further year, giving him another baby, Jane. Then her husband claimed her back. Several legitimate children followed, the Chute baptismal register describing their father as 'labourer' and 'pauper'. Elizabeth herself, at a later date, said that, in all, her family numbered eleven. One of her babies died as an infant; the progress of others is not recorded; the eldest, William, was hanged for arson. He was said to have fired a stack of corn, but as the man to whom it belonged was also one of the jury that tried him, and as, according to the rule of the day, he was not allowed to be represented but had to speak from the dock himself, his chances of being acquitted were slight. His mother never went to the trial being, as it happened, great with child, but she always swore that she knew he was innocent. It seems he was subject to epileptic fits, and when he was condemned he fainted in the dock. He was hanged in Salisbury, in 1835, and his body returned to his native parish where, on the 25th March, it was buried close to the crumbling church in a grave that is now forgotten.

1 24th November, 1817.

Perhaps because of this terrible event the Hutchins family decided to emigrate and with, presumably, the help of the parish went to America in 1836. There Charles Hutchins died, leaving Elizabeth without support. Somehow or other she managed to get back; and towards the end of 1838, then at the age of forty-four, she and her children entered the Andover Workhouse.

Known to her friends as Betty Duck—it was just, she said, the name for a fool though other people more than hinted that, for an act or two of adultery, she had earned it for being ducked in a pond—she did not prevaricate or blush for shame when McDougal asked her for a brief connexion.

Mr. McDougal made a proposal to me after I had been in the Workhouse some time; he asked me a question or two. It might be a month after I had been in the house; I was then up in the sick ward. He asked me if I had any objection to lie with him; I told him to go off. That was the first time; he asked me again afterwards. He said then the same as he said before. I considered myself, and I thought as the children were almost starved, and he said he'd give me some victuals and some beer, that if he asked me again I would.

He asked me again, and I gave consent, sir; it took place up in the sick ward. He gave me some victuals and some beer. That took place once or twice; four or five times whilst I was in the house.

There was no night in particular that it was done. There was one Saturday evening; I slept with him a little while one Saturday evening; I had a young child, and I did not stay long. He slept with me next room to mistress. He did not sleep with mistress on Saturday evenings; he slept next room to her. He did not sleep with her every Saturday evening; I know he did not then.

I recollect Mr. McDougal that evening coming up into the sick ward to me. I don't remember the time he came home, because I had been to bed, and was asleep. At that time I had a young child. He came and tapped at the door of the sick ward twice.

When he did that I went out to him; he waited till I came out. I then went down the sick-ward stairs, and

through the kitchen, and up the stairs where the master
and mistress's apartments are. I went with him to the left-
hand door; Mrs. McDougal's bed is in the right-hand door.
He slept in that room when mistress did not let him be
with she. I don't know how that was that she would not
let him be with she.

I went into that room with him about twice. I went with
him once in the sick ward; I remained some time in the
workhouse after that. The intercourse did not take place
all at one time of my being in the workhouse, but at the
different times when I was in the workhouse.

I had a baby, it was about a twelvemonth old when I
went into Mr. McDougal's bedroom. I did not dress myself
when I went down stairs, across the kitchen, and up into
Mr. McDougal's bedroom; I had only my nightgown on;
I left the baby bide in the bed. I did not sleep long with
Mr. McDougal, only a little while; I left the baby behind
me. I don't recollect there was anybody in the sick ward
but little children at that time.

I came down again the same way that I went up to his
room; I had to pass the mistress's bedroom door, both
going and returning. I had no light; I found my way because
it was not so very dark.[1]

Betty, in many respects was lucky, for at least she was able
to speak to McDougal and, when desperate, get some extras,
even although she had to pay for them. Other inmates, especially the men, simply had to live as they could, on even less, as
events were to prove, than any others of their like throughout
the country.

First of all, their official diet, that chosen by the Board of
Guardians, when they actually got it was, due to a clerical slip,
even below the basic minimum adopted in all the other workhouses. Secondly, what they usually received was even less
again than this, due to thefts committed by McDougal. He and
Mrs. McDougal together had six times a pauper's allowance but,
as his salary remained the same and, as the cost of provisions
rocketed, he began to steal the inmates' rations. He started to
skim the children's milk; illegally to vary the official diet in

1 S.C.A.U., p. 1,482.

ways that proved to his own advantage; and quite ruthlessly to take the extras, more especially beer and gin, that the doctor prescribed for the old and sick.

All the inmates who testified afterwards spoke of the terrible effects of their hunger. Many of them left, like William Newport, a man with only one leg who nevertheless had to pound bones who assuaged his hunger by gnawing candles; or Charles Lewis from Weyhill whose children survived on raw potatoes and scraps that McDougal threw to the chickens; or another pauper who dared to protest whose statement was blandly entered in the Minutes:

A complaint by Wm Brown an inmate of the Union House was heard as to not having sufficient food and wishing to leave the House and says he might as well live out with little food as in.

No shock was expressed by the Guardians or any form of inquiry instituted so that no suspicion fell on McDougal. He told the Board that the food was excellent. After all, the pressure of hunger was a necessary part of the Workhouse System. When Dodson heard that the inmates were hungry from other sources outside the Workhouse he raised his hands and eyes resignedly. Such matters were the will of God, given effect by the Poor Law Commission. Charles Lewis met him in the town and told him why he had left the Workhouse. Dodson said he was sorry to hear it; but all he did was to wish him well and urge him to bear his troubles with Christian fortitude.

In 1845, however, rumours at last began to circulate, spread by men who had left the Workhouse, which one of the Guardians, Hugh Mundy, a member of an old Andover family, a Borough Councillor and prosperous farmer—one of the few who cared for the poor and therefore one of Dodson's opponents —decided he must investigate. The stories concerned the men in the bone-yard who, it was said, were so ravenous that, in spite of the revolting smell, they were actually gnawing the bones before they broke them.

It was not long before Mundy discovered that what was rumoured was really true; many of the men to whom he spoke openly admitting that they stole the bones, even though they were green and stinking, and hid tham away to eat in the evening. The evidence of one, Samuel Green, an old lag of sixty-one who, in 1828, had been transported for seven years for stealing a kettle worth sixteen shillings and had later returned to enter the Workhouse, more than confirmed his worst suspicions.

I reside in Andover; I have no wife, but I have five children; they are all grown up and off my hands. I came into the Union Workhouse about a week after last Christmas; I went out in May; I was employed in the workhouse at bone-breaking the best part of my time; the bones were got from different parts, some from one place and some from another. There are people at Andover who collect bones. I have seen a great many marrow bones brought in; some of the marrow bones were beef, mutton, and some bacon. We looked out for the fresh bones; we used to tell the fresh bones by the look of them, and then we used to be like a parcel of dogs after them; some were not so particular about the bones being fresh as others; I like the fresh bones; I never touched one that was a little high; the marrow was as good as the meat, it was all covered over by bone, and no filth could get to it. I don't know as I ever eat a bacon marrow bone until I came into the workhouse; I found out in the workhouse that bacon marrow bones were good; I have eat meat off some of the bones; I have picked a sheep's head, a mutton bone, and a beef bone; that was when they were fresh and good; sometimes I have had one that was stale and stunk, and I eat it even then; I eat it when it was stale and stinking because I was hungered, I suppose. You see we only had bread and gruel for breakfast, and as there was no bread allowed on meat days for dinner, we saved our bread from breakfast, and then, having had only gruel for breakfast, we were hungry before dinner-time. To satisfy our hunger a little, because a pint and a half of gruel is not much for a man's breakfast, we eat the stale and stinking meat. If we could get a fresh bone we did not take the stale and stinking meat. The allowance of potatoes at dinner on meat days is half a pound, but we used to get nearly a pound, seven or eight middling sized potatoes. The food we got in the workhouse was very good; I could not wish better, all I wanted was a little more. The bread was always as good as that [*pointing to a loaf on the table*], and no man has occasion to find fault with it. The cheese was very good cheese; it has been very good for the last year or two. I have been in the workhouse once every year since the house has been opened, excepting the first year; I was in goal then; I am generally in one place or the other once a year.

I did not eat my bread any one morning in the week. I did not eat it, but not because I had too much. I used to sell it to buy a bit of 'bacco. I used to sell it in the workhouse. Most all the people who take 'bacco, sell their bread. 'Bacco is a very wholesome thing, especially in such a place as the workhouse. The fresh and stale bones used to be shot down all together. The master once found that I had saved five allowances of bread, and he took them away from me, but afterwards gave them me again. He told me he should not allow us to save bread in that way. The saving of bread used to cause a good deal of quarrelling, because some of them would steal it. I used to save a bit of bread for Sunday, because on Sundays, when you are standing about the yard doing nothing, you want more to eat than when you are working; the time seems so long when you are standing about.

I have seen a man named Reeves eat horse flesh off the bones which had been brought from Squire Smith's; I have seen him do it often. I could tell it was horse flesh by the bone. I told him it was horse flesh, but he did not care; it went down sweet as a nut. I have heard the medical officer inquire of Reeves if he had eaten horse flesh, and he . always denied it to the medical officer; but I know he did eat it, because I have seen him. Reeves was a very dirty fellow; he could not keep his clothes clean for a week; his clothes in a week would be as dirty as a chimney-sweep's. The men would not answer when Mr. Westlake, the medical officer, asked them if Reeves had eaten horse flesh. I once quarrelled with Reeves about eating it, and he asked me, 'What odds it was to me his eating of it.' I said it was no odds to me, but I could not think how he could be so nasty as to eat such stuff.

I recollect Mr. Westlake, Mr. Hugh Mundy, and Mr.

Loscombe, coming into the day-room, and having the
men round them to inquire whether it was true such stuff
had been eaten. The men said they had not seen him eat
horse flesh; but I told Reeves I had seen him eat it. Upon
that Mr. Mundy shook his head, and turned himself round,
and the gentlemen went away after that. The horse bones
from Squire Smith's are boiled. I never saw anyone but
Reeves and Eaton eat horse flesh. I once saw Eaton take up
a horse's leg, and take the hair off it, and eat the flesh.
The leg was not cooked. No one saw him eat it but me.
Eaton is weak in his intellect, and I don't think he has got
any taste, or smell either. I have often seen the governor
give Eaton extra food when he has not given it to other
inmates.[1]

The mark X of *Samuel Green*

Whatever McDougal had done for Eaton, Mundy felt, when
he heard this story and similar disclosures from other inmates,
that the pounding of bones had got to be stopped; and having
only a fortnight earlier failed to carry a motion at the Board
that the pounding of bones should be discontinued, the last
of many similar attempts since the grinding of bones had
started in the Workhouse, he decided to take up the matter
himself and write to his Member of Parliament.

For some reason the summer passed before the latter took
any action, but just before the session closed, one of the
foremost Poor Law critics, John Wakley, the Member for
Finsbury, a friend of Cobbett's and fearless reformer who was
also a friend of the Member for Andover, raised the matter in
the House of Commons and asked whether it was really true
that the Andover paupers were gnawing bones.

The Home Secretary, Sir James Graham, dismissed the
story as being absurd but promised to ask the Poor Law
Commission to send an Assistant to Andover immediately.
The latter arrived on the 3rd of August, went at once to the
Workhouse bone-yard, and questioned Eaton and several
others. What they told him, then and later, freed at last from
the threats of McDougal, was soon to be published throughout

1 S.C.A.U., p. 1,336

the country. For a week, however, nothing happened. The Assistant Commissioner returned to London. McDougal behaved as brutally as ever. The Guardians met and shrugged their shoulders. Then a public inquiry was ordered; and every single terrible rumour was found to be true.

Chapter 9

THE FACTS THAT thus were revealed at Andover, every single
one of which, laid before the Assistant Commissioner at the
public inquiry held in the town, was reported in detail, daily, in
The Times, at long last produced the wave of shock, horror and
disgust that John Walter and all his supporters had sought to
arouse for years.

As soon as Parliament reassembled—in January 1846—
Ralph Etwall, the Member for Andover, raised the matter in
the House of Commons and asked for a Select Committee of
Inquiry. For apart from the Workhouse scandal itself, the
manner in which it had been investigated had given rise to a
scandal, too. The Assistant Commissioner who had undertaken
it, a man named Henry Walter Parker, had been none other
than the same Assistant who had held the Inquiry at the
Brackley Workhouse where the little boy had been scalded to
death and who, later, in spite of this accident, had recommended the master, Howe, to the post of the master of the workhouse at Eton. Hard enough though it is to believe, his judgement had failed him again at Andover in almost exactly similar
circumstances. Apart from holding the investigation in a very
partial and impudent manner, excusing McDougal whenever
he could and interrupting and bullying the witnesses he had,
when McDougal decided to retire to avoid the shame of public
dismissal, recommended a man named Price, formerly master of
the workhouse at Oxford who, too, had just resigned for the
same reason—to avoid dismissal—on being accused of inhumanity. Parker had pleaded ignorance of this, but the Poor
Law Commissioners, thoroughly annoyed had, in turn, told
Parker to retire (again, to avoid a public dismissal) feeling,
with understandable annoyance, *The Times* and public opinion

against them, that McDougal and the bones were troubles enough without the addition of a careless Assistant.

Parker, however, had felt aggrieved, and after publishing in self defence the complete series of letters and replies which had passed between himself and the Commission—a volume of almost sixty pages—he had sent a petition to the House of Commons praying that his case should be investigated.

He would not in the ordinary way have succeeded, but his plea was just the excuse that was wanted by all those who hated the Poor Law to widen the scope of the Committee of Inquiry to include the work of the whole Commission; so luckily for him his request was granted. Lastly, Sir James Graham himself, by trying to belittle the Andover scandal and calling it a 'mere workhouse squabble' which, at a time of national crisis—the Commons were then debating the corn laws—ought not to be wasting a minute of their time, made an Inquiry a virtual certainty.

On the 5th of March, 1846, the following motion received a majority:

> *Ordered*, That a Select Committee be appointed to inquire into the Administration of the Poor Laws in the Andover Union, and also into the Management of the Union Workhouse; and into the Conduct of the Poor-law Commissioners, and their late Assistant Commissioner, Mr. Parker, in reference to the Two Investigations held at Andover; and into all the Circumstances under which the Poor-law Commissioners called upon Mr. Parker to resign his Assistant Commissionership.

The Times reported the fact in triumph. To those who worked in the Poor Law Commission it sounded the knell of doom.

For unknown to the general public (although, of course, rumoured in Westminster) apart from the trials of unpopularity —and no men in public life had been more abused than those in the Commission—conflicts within the office itself, between the Secretary, Chadwick, and the Board, had long divided the staff into camps and created almost unworkable conditions. No proper meetings of the Board had been held for nearly five years, and decisions, frequently of vital importance about, for instance, the pounding of bones and the institution of the Prohibitory Order, had been made at times by one Commissioner, unrecorded in official minutes, and often taken quite regardless of the natural meaning and spirit of the law.

The trouble had lain with the organisation as first set up in 1834. Chadwick had wanted to be a Commissioner, and having been one of the panel of advisers who had done the initial survey of the Poor Law and recommended the Workhouse System as the quickest method of setting it to rights, and having seen his proposal adopted, his hope of appointment had not been unreasonable. He was, however, an intellectual, and also, socially, not well born. Lord Melbourne, the Home Secretary, whose task it had been to make the appointment, detested theorists in any capacity; he had also felt, with a certain justice, given the code in practice at the time, that all the Commissioners ought to be 'gentlemen'. He had, therefore, refused to nominate him; instead, had only appointed him Secretary; and in so doing, making a compromise which had led, predictably, to jealousy and conflict. For Chadwick, then aged 34, lately Jeremy Bentham's secretary, highly intelligent and conscientious but also humourless and introspective, had accepted the post with a sense of grievance; and when, in 1839, he had failed again to be appointed when one of the Commissioners had decided to retire, he had not been able to control his bitterness. He ought, of course, to have given in his notice; instead he had grimly stuck to his post, behaving, generally, with obstructive silence, daring any of the Board to sack him, sometimes declining to accept instructions if he thought them contrary to Poor Law doctrine. The Board, already harassed by *The Times*, and wishing to avoid the extra attention that any dismissal was bound to bring—for Chadwick, roused, was sure to be difficult and certain to seek the maximum publicity—had weakly decided to ignore the issue. Hoping, finally, to freeze him out they had simply conducted their work without him, including even their formal meetings. Such a course had been highly improper. Now, with a Parliamentary Committee of Inquiry, their every act and every motive would stand publicly revealed.

Contrary to normal practice today, the Committee conducted its business in public so that all that was said and revealed before them was reported almost daily in the press. All the

Commission's troubles were told; the saga, too, of Parker's dismissal; also the history of Andover Workhouse—Dodson, Mundy, Cooke, McDougal, thirty other local inhabitants as well as more than a dozen paupers (to the great delight of all the newsmen) all appearing at the House of Commons to give their evidence in person.

In a last great series of dispatches *The Times* reported every detail, day after day in column after column, culled from nearly fifty sittings, couched in terms of triumph and delight, sure, now, that the battle was won, the Poor Law Commission certain of removal.

The fate of the Poor Law Commission is sealed [the editor wrote, in the middle of July]. We cannot imagine what justification the Government can find for hesitating a single day to get rid of the Poor Law Commissioners . . . The Poor Law Commission has burst like a shell . . . Somerset House is in the air, and Commissioners, secretaries, Dukes, Ministers, things great and small, are tumbling down, rather the worse for their forced aerial expedition.

The Andover Union Committee begins to acquire a tragic interest. In the present dearth of the legitimate drama, we know not where better materials or, we may add, better acting, are to be found. It is there that we must look for the true revelations of London. For these twelve years we have been pumping in vain for a moderate amount of disclosure. We now almost tremble at the excessive result of our own curiosity. It is like an Artesian well in which you dig right down for half a mile, and at the end of two years and a half find yourself one fine morning spirited up to the clouds . . . The whole Commission is now booked for ages of notoriety.[1]

In the customary huge, unmanageable volumes the Committee published their report in August with twenty thousand questions and answers forming a thousand pages of evidence to which were added thirty appendices on every aspect of workhouse life including Parker's original report on the gnawing of

1 15th July, 4.e.; 4th August., 4.d.; 13th August, 4.b.; 20th August, 4.b.

bones and McDougal's indecencies. It contained, predictably, many criticisms.

That Mr. McDougal's conduct while Master of the Workhouse was marked by undue severity; that he was on several occasions, once even when reading prayers to the inmates, seen in a state of intoxication; that he was utterly deficient in many of the qualities which are of essential importance in the difficult position which he filled, viz. fairness and impartiality, a due sense of truth, a well-regulated temper, and proper habits of self-control.

That, without going further in this place into details, for which they refer to the Evidence and Papers printed herewith, the Committee feel bound, upon the evidence given before them, to express their conviction of the utter unfitness of Mr. McDougal and his wife for the situations of master and matron, which they respectively held from December 1836 to September 1845, and they have therefore learned, with much astonishment, that his influence with the Board has been far greater than that which should properly belong to his office, and the confidence reposed in him seems to have been unqualified.

That the bad administration of the Andover Workhouse, and the rigor with which the Board of Guardians, generally acting in accordance with the frequently published views of the Poor-law Commissioners, have carried out the law, have often been the means of inducing labourers to accept reduced wages in order to avoid the workhouse.

That, whatever feelings the Commissioners may have entertained with regard to Mr. Parker's mode of conducting the Andover Inquiry, or his defective superintendence of the Andover Union, the time and the manner of Mr. Parker's removal from his office appear to them, after full consideration of the whole case, to have been such as to give him just cause of complaint, and to have been inconsistent with a discreet exercise of that power of dismissing their subordinate officers which the law has entrusted to the Commissioners.

That on a review of the proceedings of the Commissioners with respect to the Andover Inquiries, and towards Mr. Parker . . ., it appears that they have been irregular and arbitrary, not in accordance with the Statute under which they exercise their functions, and such as to shake public confidence in their administration of the law.[1]

The Times reported the findings simply; for although the Commission had still a year before its current term expired—the five years' continuation granted in 1842—its end had now become a certainty, and nothing further could be gained by comment.

Thus, in July 1847, after a reign of thirteen years, the Poor Law Commission finally expired, hounded to death by public opinion—by the outrage felt by ordinary people against a dictatorial junta whose powers to oppress the starving poor had been used with heartless, doctrinal, severity—for whom, luckily, the owner of *The Times* had become the champion and dedicated spokesman.

In the same week, Walter died, *The Times* carrying the sombre news in an issue entirely edged in black. His monument today remains his newspaper which, in the course of fifty years (he died at the age of seventy-one), he raised from the status of an ordinary journal, indistinguishable from a dozen others, to that of the greatest oracle in Europe, a paper whose influence could not be bought, or voice of criticism curbed or softened. This achievement and many others: that of the use of the power of steam which, when first applied to printing, increased the hourly number of copies from a mere three hundred when pulled by hand to twelve hundred when produced by machinery; that of his natural aptitude for business; that of his instinctive sense of news; that of his choice of brilliant editors; are all still rightly remembered while, because the Poor Law has gone, his fight against it is largely forgotten.

For those, however, who composed his obituary it figured amongst his greatest successes.

> Mr. Walter happily lived long enough to see his principles confirmed by the most cogent historical demonstrations . . .
> His public spirit was not of that exclusive or theoretical character which comprehends only a class or a constituency

1 S.C.A.U. Report, 20th August, 1846.

within the range of its affections . . . He considered every Englishman his fellow-citizen and friend, and sought the suffrage of affection from the humblest labourer, and the feeblest and most desolate pauper as anxiously as the vote and interest of the all-important elector. They only who knew Mr. Walter can be aware how much his feelings for the poor had been formed and cherished by the associations of his personal experience, and how much the bereavements, the separations, the denials, and indignities from which he sought to rescue the unprivileged and persecuted classes of this country, were those which he had personally felt or witnessed or both . . . His indignation at the injustice and cruelty done to the poor by a notorious act, and at the triumphant tone of its advocates in Parliament hurried him again into harassing, tedious and expensive contests. It was his desire to re-enter the House of Commons . . . armed with a public commission to throw back in the face of the Minister the oft repeated vaunt that the Poor Law was acceptable to the people of England. Time, however, reserved his triumph. The verdict of England reached Mr. Walter in the chamber of death. It was there that he heard the fate of the once potent Commission . . . He died with the news of victory in his ear.[1]

1 29th July, 1847.

F

Chapter 10

LIFE IN THE Workhouse after the tempest which broke over it so unexpectedly and gave Andover a greater publicity than any enjoyed for a hundred years, since the finest days of the Weyhill Fair, continued nevertheless for the inmates in every respect as grimly as ever. The Guardians, of course, continued to meet and their Minutes reveal some irritable tremors, but on the whole they kept their heads and merely, firmly, bowed them to the storm. Colin McDougal eventually resigned—Dodson positively refused to sack him—and his letter is faithfully preserved in their proceedings.

Andover   Septr 20th 1845

Gentlemen

A letter received yesterday morning from the Poor Law Commissioners, of which you have a copy has induced my legal advisers, to recommend me thus to resign the office of Master & Matron of the Andover Union Workhouse, which offices I & my wife have filled from the formation of the Union, so as to meet the repeated approbation of yourselves and the Guardians your predecessors.

The circumstances which have led to this resignation, must be known to all of you & I have no hesitation in stating that it is no consciousness of inability on my own part, or that of my legal advisers to meet the charges so industriously collected against me, in such a manner as to justify a continuance of the confidence so long reposed in me by every one of those whose good opinion I value, but because the hasty and unexpected resumption of the Inquiry notwithstanding the adjournment granted by the Assistant Commissioner & acceded to by the Counsel for the Prosecution, has wholly deprived me of the means of laying my defence before you and the public in a satisfactory manner.

I really do not know how to express my feelings for the kindness you have shewn me during the progress of the persecution which has for some time passed [*sic*] raged against me, but you may be assured I shall always remember it with thankfulness and gratitude.

I only wait your nomination of persons to take the situations now vacant to whom I may as soon as convenient resign your accounts, stores, etc. etc. in such a state as may be most satisfactory to you & me.

Gentlemen I remain
Your faithful & most grateful Servant
Colin McDougal[1]

Union Workhouse
Andover.

The Guardians accepted his resignation, the more cheerfully when they discovered that Price whom Parker recommended— the former Oxford workhouse master—had himself been in similar difficulties and could, therefore, on equal grounds be claimed by themselves to be unacceptable. Then they selected a man named Blyth, a prison officer from Parkhurst gaol. He held the post for three years until he, too, was given notice for taking liberties with female inmates. Who succeeded him does not concern us. Troubles, however, continued for many years.

Parker, too, wrote on his departure, addressing himself to the Clerk to the Union.

Highgate. 22nd October 1845

My dear Sir.

The Poor Law Commissioners having requested me to send in my resignation, though at the same time they assure me they have taken such step with the utmost reluctance, and acknowledge the zealous and efficient services which I have on various occasions rendered to the Commission, I have been constrained to resign my office,

---

1 He retired to Dundee and died in 1864, aged seventy-one.

and the Commissioners have fixed such resignation to take effect from the 31st instant.

As my official connection with the Union will thus almost suddenly cease, I shall feel extremely obliged to you to communicate this information to the Guardians at their next meeting, and express to them my acknowledgement of the attention and courtesy with which they have ever received my suggestions.

In requesting you to make this communication to the Board, I cannot refrain from assuring you of the grateful remembrance in which I shall ever hold your prompt and kind attentions to me.

I remain

My dear Sir

Yours very truly

H. W. Parker[1]

Thos. Lamb Esq.

Christopher Dodson also resigned, at the next annual election of Guardians, although in fact, as a Justice of the Peace, he was ex officio a member of the Board. He, too, wrote to Lamb.

Penton.   April 8. 1847

My dear Sir.

As a new Board of Guardians is now elected, they will of course proceed to the Election of a Chairman—and as during the last twelve years, the successive Boards of Guardians have unanimously elected me to that office, I think it right to state at once that it is not my intention (should the present Board of Guardians pay me a similar compliment) to take upon myself the office.

It is not (believe me) without much regret that I leave a situation, in which whatever may have been my deficiencies I have endeavoured fearlessly to do what I have considered right. It is not without much regret that I break a connection with men with whom I shall ever feel proud to have been associated, and by whom I trust I shall ever be con-

1 H.R.O. 64.M.48. 21/3. Four years later Parker emigrated to South Australia where, at the bar, 'as a criminal pleader he especially excelled'. He died in 1874 at the age of sixty-five. (*South Australian Register* 28/3/74.)

sidered as a friend. My warmest thanks are due to them, but I do feel that the proper time for my retirement is arrived.

In making you the organ of this communication I cannot omit the opportunity of thanking you personally for the courtesy and attention you have ever exercised towards me. With sincerest wishes for increased prosperity to the Union, and with an heartfelt prayer for the real happiness and comfort of every individual comprised in it—Believe me always

My Dear Sir,
Yrs most truly
Ch^r Dodson[1]

Thos Lamb Esq

In spite of Dodson's benevolent wishes, little occurred in the Andover Union to bring them to any practical fulfilment.

For instance, details survive in the Minutes of the case of a labourer, William Few, a one-legged man from Faccomb, a hamlet ten miles from Andover, who with his wife and three children walked to the Workhouse in the depth of winter, there to be cruelly refused admittance because, legally, he was not a pauper. Few complained to his local Guardian who sent the case to the Poor Law Commissioners. They posted back a long epistle containing all the technical data on when a man might be deemed to be destitute and therefore entitled to relief by right, but refused to comment on Few's complaint which, they held, was a local matter. The Guardians blandly filed the advice and waited for Few to apply again. Understandably, he never did so. How he lived can only be imagined. Even people inside the Workhouse were suffering from hunger as badly as ever. Once again the rations had been cut; and every promise of improved conditions had, in only a matter of months, been quietly laid aside.

For while, after the scandal of the bones, the inmates' diet had been augmented—the children having extra milk, the adults extra bread and vegetables and, as a further treat on Sundays, a special allowance of suet pudding—an unexpected national crisis enabled the Guardians again to reduce it.

1 Union Minutes, 10th April, 1847.

In the autumn of 1845 potatoes were struck by a strange disease which turned them to black, inedible pulp. Within a year there was widespread hunger—in Ireland conditions of actual famine—in spite of the abolition of the corn laws. As well as this, a terrible winter led to general unemployment. The Andover Workhouse was jammed to capacity, the cost of running it more than doubled. The Board resolved that in these conditions the amended diet was 'too liberal'; so once more, for the sake of the ratepayers, they ruthlessly cut it down.

Once again the Guardian for Andover, still the friend and champion of the inmates but also now, for having stood up for them and bringing to light the matter of the bones, the most unpopular man in the district, tried for a moment to improve their lot.

> Mr. Hugh Mundy proposed that as Christmas Day falls on Friday, a Bread and Cheese Day, and as no subscription could be raised to give the inmates Roast Beef and plum puddings on that day, the diet for Tuesday consisting of meat, etc. be substituted for that of Friday. Which proposition was not seconded.

This was the Christmas of 1846, the one preceding Dodson's retirement. It seemed that the 'current of private charity', of which he had boasted in 1836, that never had it run so clearly as after the introduction of the Workhouse, had now, after the revelations, frozen completely at source.

In fact, if anything, after the Inquiry and after the demise of the Poor Law Commission, life in the Workhouse rapidly deteriorated. The Guardians never forgave the paupers for having complained about the bones and for having exposed them to public censure, and once the clouds had blown away they began to oppress them as brutally as ever. The pounding of bones, of course, had been stopped; throughout the country as well as in Andover. Flints were procured for the Workhouse instead which, if anything, were even worse as *in extremis* they could not be eaten.

If the inmates thought that the Poor Law Board which took over the reins from the hated Commission and had, as Secretary, a Junior Minister, having a seat in the House of Commons and being, therefore, subject to control, was going to help them improve their lot they soon discovered they were quite mistaken. The third volume of the Guardians' Minutes which opens in July, 1847, in the week, as it happened, of Walter's death and also that of the Poor Law Commission, reveals that life inside the Workhouse was, if possible, worse than before.

In the last half of this year the Porter was sacked for 'exposing his person'; the Master was accused of immorality; the Workhouse was described as 'very disorderly' and rife with measles and influenza; the diet was said to be 'not sufficient'; the Guardians were rebuked by Parker's successor who was now entitled a Poor Law Inspector and asked to hold an immediate inquiry.

Even the Minutes looked the same as they had done right from the very beginning. Still they were signed by Christopher Dodson. His resignation had come as a shock, and in the end had not been accepted as no one else had been willing to replace him.

So, once more, he had agreed to serve; and in the summer of 1847, at a moment as pleasant as any in his life, only surpassed in 1839 when his friends had given him the massive epergne as a mark of esteem for his work as Chairman, he had ridden back to the Andover Workhouse. Precisely, thereafter, at ten o'clock on Saturday the 24th of April, he had entered the Boardroom, bowed to the Clerk, smiled at the Guardians and resumed his seat. He remained an active Chairman of the Board up to the very end of his days. In April, 1876, he died at the age of eighty-three, having served the ratepayers for forty years and attended over two thousand meetings.

The Board, in fact, became Dodson's life. Its Minutes, faithfully preserving its work, better than any marble slab, record his troubled times and form his epitaph.

Appendices

APPENDIX A

Guardians present at first meeting
11th July 1835

Ex Officio Guardians	*Status or profession*
Sir John Walter Pollen	Baronet M.P.
William Iremonger	Esquire
Charles Gardiner	Major
Revd. Christopher Dodson	Clerk
Henry Gawler	Esquire
Edward Dyke Poore	Esquire
William Fowle Junr.	Esquire

	Elected Guardians	*Rank or Status*
Andover	Hugh Mundy	Gentleman
	William Langstaff	Chemist
	James Baker	Carrier
	Joseph Wakeford	Mealman
	Thomas Heath	Banker
Foxcott	Henry Sweetapple	
Penton Mewsey	John Ward	
Penton Grafton	Hugh Stacpoole	Esquire
Appleshaw	George Redman	Farmer
Knights Enham	Samuel Guyatt	
Tangley	George Young	Insurance Agent
Chute	Henry Bethell	Gentleman
Chute Forest	Samuel Harrison	
Hurstbourne Tarrant	Robert Holdway	
Vernhams Deane	Hiram Bull	Yeoman
Linkenholt	Richard Osmond	

155

Faccomb	Stephen Collier	
Abbotts Ann	Thomas Wise	
Longparish	Revd. Henry B. Greene	Clerk
Bullington	Anthony Paice	
Barton Stacey	William Courtney Sr.	
Wherwell	James Forder	
Goodworth Clatford	Thomas Dowling	Yeoman
Upper Clatford	John Lywood	Yeoman
Chilbolton	Henry Tredgold	
Thruxton	Harry Noyes	Gentleman
Fifield	Henry Stephen Sutton	
Amport	William Dowling	Yeoman
Monxton	James Soper	
Quarley	Jacob Crook	
Grately	William Henry Gale	Gentleman
Shipton	Daniel Chandler	
Kimpton	George Ralph Gale	Gentleman
Tidworth North	Thomas B. Northeast	Gentleman
Tidworth South	William Dowling	Yeoman
Ludgershall	Jacob Crook	Farmer

APPENDIX B

Robert Cooke's daily round as described by himself in a letter to the Poor Law Commissioners, 14th August, 1837. (P.R.O. M.H. 12/10661.)

August, 1837

Routine of Relieving Officer for Districts No. 1 and 4 consolidated—

Monday. Attends at the Workhouse to Register Births and Deaths that may have occurred since the previous Saturday, to receive applications for relief from paupers belonging to Andover and afterwards goes into Town and visits paupers receiving relief on account of sickness and collects silver (a task of no small difficulty) to pay the paupers in the country on the two following days—

Tuesday. Pays the paupers of Monxton at nine o'clock in the morning at a paupers house, the contractor delivers the bread out of his cart at the same time at the door. Goes on to Amport where the paupers are paid in the same way with the exception of two who are paid at their own houses and the bread and money for four is left at the village shop. Goes from Amport to Thruxton; here there is no station but the paupers are paid at their own houses—goes from Thruxton to Quarley where the paupers assemble at a paupers house—goes on from Quarley to Grately where the paupers are few and each one is called on and paid—at each of the Parishes paid this day the contractor delivers the Bread out of his cart at the same time that the paupers receive their money.

The Relieving Officer commences at Monxton every week at the same time and arrives in the other parishes about the same hour every week. He takes applications for relief and visits the sick in each parish as he goes through and arrives at home generally about 4 o'clock in the afternoon the remainder of the day is occupied in making the requisite entries in the Relief List of the several Parishes paid this day.

Wednesday. Pays the Paupers of Kimpton at 9 o'clock in the morning at a Paupers house, here the Bread is delivered by a person who supplies it for the contractor to the paupers at 4 o'clock in the afternoon of this day. Goes on from Kimpton to Snoddington to a Baker who supplies a part of the bread for the Contractor this person sends his cart with the Bread required to a Public House at Shipton where the paupers are paid and receive the Bread out of the cart at the door. Goes on from Shipton to South Tedworth where the paupers are paid at a Paupers House and the Bread delivered out of the cart at the door—goes from South Tedworth to North Tedworth where the paupers are paid in the same way as at South Tedworth. Goes on to Ludgershall where the paupers are paid at the House of the person who supplied the Bread for the contractor —they receive the Bread at the same time as they are paid the money at this place—goes from Ludgershall to Fifield where the paupers assemble at a paupers house the Bread is generally delivered at this place about the same time as the money is paid.

The Relieving Officer commences at Kimpton at the same hour every week and arrives in the other Parishes for this day about the same hour and visits the sick and takes applications in the same way as on Tuesday and arrives at home about the same hour and occupies the remainder of the day in the same way.

Thursday. Leaves home at 8 o'clock in the morning, passes through Foxcott at ½ past 8, pays Ann Spreadbury the only pauper who resides in the Parish and arrives at Enham Church at 9 o'clock where the Bread had been delivered in the Porch about 10 minutes. Pays the paupers of this Parish and goes on to the Workhouse—goes into the Town and collects silver and copper and commences paying at the Workhouse the paupers of Andover at 11 o'clock the bread having been delivered this morning into the Relieving Officers Room is handed to each pauper as they are paid the money by a pauper of the House under the eye of the Relieving Officer.

The payment of the paupers occupies generally until half past 12 o'clock when applications are received and entered in the application Book and those received in the country parishes up to this time are also entered. Births & Deaths that have occurred since Monday are Registered. Applicants for relief who reside in the Town and persons receiving relief on account of sickness are visited at their own homes this occupies the remainder of this day.

Friday. In the morning (if time was wanting the day before) enters the several parishes paid in the Relief List; at 10 o'clock pays the paupers of Penton Mewsey in the Church Porch where the bread has been previously deposited—at one o'clock pays the paupers of Penton Grafton at my own house where the Bread has been previously delivered—at three o'clock pays the paupers of Appleshaw at the Church where the Bread has been previously delivered visits the sick in these several Parishes makes up the weeks account and generally has this evening to go into some of the parishes to visit bad cases of sickness.

Saturday. Arrives at the Workhouse at 9 o'clock in the morning; enters in the Receipt Expenditure Book (this being a large Book is always kept at the House) the Receipts and payments of the past week and lays the whole of the Books before the Clerk (who shortly after arrives) for his inspection.

The whole of this day is occupied in attending the Board of Guardians, in paying the relief ordered by them this day to the paupers of Andover, in visiting paupers at their houses and in Registering Births & Deaths that have occurred since Thursday—

Sunday. A portion of this day is often occupied in visiting sick paupers or in preparing papers called for by the Board of Guardians—

The arrangements as far as regards the stations in the several Parishes forming what was lately District No. 4 was made previous to my having charge of that District. I disapproved of them in some of the Parishes and stated so to the Board after my first visit.

R. Cook

APPENDIX C

Letters to the Poor Law Commissioners

1. From Leonard Lywood and William Horwood (P.R.O. M.H. 12/10661)
2. From William Grosse (P.R.O. M.H. 25/2)

Poor Law Commissioners for England and Wales.

Gentlemen,

I trouble you with this if not for the recovery of what I consider I am entitled to at least for the interpretation of the 54 Sec. of the Act which authorises the overseers to give relief in cases of sudden and urgent necessity. As overseer of Barton Stacey in the county of Hants I was applied to by a woman for relief, her husband having been imprisoned the previous day she stated she had no means of obtaining any bread and had not sufficient for herself and children *for the day* of course I do not think that an overseer under such circumstances ought to turn the woman with two children away to become beggars until she could meet with the relieving officer. I therefore gave her a gallon of bread it being on a *Sunday* and told her to apply to the relieving officer on the following Tuesday when he came round. I presented the relieving officer with the account to lay before the Board of Guardians and by them it was refused. I should feel obliged if you would favour with a reply if I have exceeded the duty of an overseer or if I am entitled to be reimbursed the small pittance, it is not the amount that I feel anxious about but am anxious as far as I can scrupulously to fulfil my duty.

I am, Gentlemen,
Your Obt. and humle. Sert.
Leonard Lywood

Overseer
Barton Stacey
Union of Andover
August 21st 1839.

161

Poor Law Commissioners of England and Wales

Gentlemen,

I beg to call attention to my letter of the 21st August 1839 as overseer of Barton Stacey, county of Hants, Union of Andover respecting the refusal of the Board of Guardians to allow me the amount for a gallon of bread given to a poor woman with two children. If necessary I will produce the pauper who will state on oath that if I had not given her the relief I did they must have starved having spent her last halfpenny that morning for milk for her children and had not more that a $\frac{1}{4}$ of a lb. of bread left. The shop keeper refusing to trust her, her husband being much in debt there it might also be proper to state her husband was imprisoned quite unexpectedly the day before. I do not wish to be troublesome but am aware you have had communication with the Board of Guardians on the subject I should feel obliged by your giving me your opinion thereon so that I may be enabled to guide my future conduct as overseer thereby.

I am, Gentlemen, you Humb. Sevt.
Leonard Lywood

Barton Stacey
September 16th 1839

The Poor Law Commissioners for England and Wales

Gentlemen,

I have received a letter from your Secretary requesting me to state on what grounds I refused relief to the wife of Isaac Barter, my reasons were as follows. When Isaac Barter and his wife went from our village on Saturday morning to appear before the Magistrates at Andover they did not know but they should both return to their home in the evening. On Mrs. Barter's return before she had been to her home she applied to me for relief. I told her that I was not justified in relieving her as she must have the same quantity of provisions in her house now for herself that she and her husband would have had if he had returned with her and if he had returned it was not likely that they would have applied for relief. On this the woman made use of some expressions that I disapproved of. I told her to apply to Mr. Richard King, her husband's Master and *gentleman farmer* who her husband had been to work for that week. She would have had about one mile to have walked to his house. She said that he was gone to market. I told her that she should have stated her case to the relieving officer or the Guardian as they were in Andover at the time she was, as I could not relieve her I told her that she had better state her case to the relieving office on the following Tuesday and that he would take her case to the Board of Guardians. On the Tuesday she applied to the relieving officer and he took her case. I was present at the time on the same day she applied to Mr. Richard King who gave her 7s 6d in part of the money due to her husband. This Gentlemen, is the case as it occurred. I exceedingly regret that such a case should have come before you. It is calculated I perceive to sever that bond of friendship that has for many years subsisted between Mr. Leonard Lywood and me which I anxiously wish to avoid and I beg further to observe that it would give more satisfaction to the ratepayers and the receivers if the overseers were invested with more extensive power than they now are. It will prevent unpleasant communications and will also prevent these degrading epithets that are so often applied by the poor on those who have anything to do under this new Law particularly in the Rural Districts, in fact it is impossible wholly to comply with the rules in the Rural District.

I remain your obedient Servant
William Horwood
Overseer of Barton Stacey

Barton Stacey
September 27 1839

Poor Law Commissioners for England and Wales

Newton Stacey
April 5 1840

Gentlemen,

I trust you will not think me too troublesome but I must call your attention to the last letter I received from you of the 5th October 1839 and numbered as above wherein you confirmed to me as to relief granted as overseer and which my fellow overseer did not, as I requested him, enter it in the quarterly account and now that it is introduced and the auditor (who I suppose anticipated it from the Board of Guardians having given the Clerk orders to *watch* it) has sent me a special summons to attend, now I have had nothing whatever to do with the money or accounts nor is it customary for more than one to attend but this is evidently done for the purpose of getting some pleasurable excuse to deny me that trifling sum. I must therefore Gentlemen request that you will favour me with a reply to confirm your previous decision by giving a positive order of payment[1] and not subject me to the loss of a day of valuable time and expense for the sake of substantiating my just claim of twenty pence.

> I am Gentlemen
> Your Obt. humle. servant
> Leonard Lywood

Parish of Barton Stacey
Union of Andover.

> To the Honorable
> The Board of Commissionars
> of the Poor-Laws, etc.

Gentlemen,

Having several times seen an exposure, in the public papers, of the system Italian organ players persue, by which they draw large sums in voluntary gifts from the public, it occurs to me that this channel of willing charity might be turned into a public benefice, namely: either for the amelioration of the contition of the parish poor or for to diminish the rates of poor housekeepers. Therefore I beg humbly to suggest: that persons [paupers] should be sent out from workhouses with barrel instruments not only of a better quality but also in better tune as those now heard in the streets accompanyed by a lad or lads with locked mony boxes for collecting whatever the public ofers; a woman or man or young persons with good voices for singing songs, set on the barrels, and an orderly person selling music in prints when asked for alltogether four persons, would

1 The Poor Law Commissioners declined to do so, and Lywood lost his money.

be necessary as complement for one organ on wheels, and these ought to be under the surveillance of the police for obvious reasons.

The question now arises, where is the mony to come from to defray the expences of the barrel instruments, engraving and printing music? I beg leave to answer thus: There should be a licencing office for intinnerant musician in general; and the italian masters of street organ players, I should make them pay for every man or boy they send out, ten shillings per months, which from the profits they derived from vagabondism, they can well afford. Suppose 500 organs are sent out by those Italians, the amount would be in one month 250 pounds for which at least 12 instruments of superior quality might be bought as an experiment for a populous and extensive parish. However it would be advisable to be secretly in preparation every part of the scheme till complete.

I am now going to show the incalculable profit which would arise from the sale of printed music for the Piano Forte, flute etc. such as is to be made public through the medium of barrel instruments, for which I take the liberty of craving your kind indulgence.

Per examble; a set of Quadrilles requiring six music plates of metal and one for the fiddle would cost, engraving and all, about £2.0.0. from which 1500 to 2000 copies might be printed of. Each 100 copies would cost in paper and printing together at the highest £1.4.0. A single copy if marked at 2d. only, for cheapness sake, if sold at full price would amount to £10.0.0. per hundred so, that paper and printing deducted, a clear profit of £8.10.0. would accrue. But then the music shops are accustomed to pay only half price to each other, the medium would be therefore between 6 and 7 pound which however is difficult to guess exactly. Now as there can be at least 10 tunes on each barrels and supposing one parish sending out six of them dayly, some playing songs, accompanyed be a good voice, some dances, some sacred music etc. 60 tunes, choise ones of curse, would invite numerous performers on musical instruments to buy and if only six out of this sixty should become favorites the desire of possessing them would soon spread over the united Kingdom, especially if such favorites through the medium of an head office in London should be made heard in every great town of the empire, then could it not fail, orders from every point of the compass would flow in; for which and in order to execute them, a shop, no need of being elegant and high rented, should be established in some spot of London convenient for the trade; to whom it would be a new source of profit, therefore musicsellers would have no cause of complaint. As to the italians no right is taken away from them and for that reason it would not be necessary to apply for an act of parliament to licence them. In my opinion it would be an act of internal policy only, justifiabel in the view of a great public good; as it is probable that many thousands of pounds might yearly be raised from a willing and charitable people without vexatious compulsion especially if confidence is established by giving the parish overseers authority of (not being debarred) of auditing the accounts.

Praying the Honerable board will excuse the writing of an old man who seldom writes so much, I leave my proposal to their more enlightened discernment in deciding the question: 'Is it wise or not to turn a profitable stream *running waste*, for a good purpose?'

> Most respectfully
> Your

devout and obedt. Servt.
Wm. Grosse

13, Warwick St.
Belgrave Road Pimlico
21st Sept. 1843

Organist at the German Lutheran
Church, Savoy. 32 years in London.

Bibliography

BIBLIOGRAPHY

		Abbreviation
	Source	*in footnotes*[1]
1.	The Public Record Office	P.R.O.
	The Ministry of Health papers	M.H.
	The Home Office papers	H.O.
	The Treasury papers	T.
	The Assize papers	A.
2.	The Hampshire Record Office	H.R.O.
	The Andover Union papers.	

3. The British Museum, State Paper Room.
   The Select Committee on Andover
   Union, 1846   S.C.A.U.
   The Report on the Poor Law Commissioners on the
   continuation of the Poor Law Commission, 1840.
   The Select Committees on the Poor Law Amendment
   Act, 1837/38.
   The Report and Appendices of H.M. Commission for
   enquiring into the Administration and Practical Opera-
   tion of the Poor Laws, 1834.
   Extracts from the above Report, 1837. (From p. 336 of
   which is taken the letter from the Revd. H. H. Milman to
   Edwin Chadwick, quoted at the beginning of this book.)
4. The University of London
   Nassau Senior's MSS Diary of the passing of the Poor
   Law Amendment Act, 1834,
   Alice May Colson's thesis: 'The revolt of the Hampshire
   Agricultural Labourers, 1937.'

1 The abbreviation q.p. after a reference indicates that the document is
only quoted in part.

5. University College, London
   The Chadwick papers.

6. The University of Nottingham
   The Bentinck papers.

7. General
   The State of the Poor, F. M. Eden, 1797.
   A History of the English Poor Law, G. Nicholls, 1860.
   The Village Labourer, J. L. & B. Hammond, 1911.
   English Poor Law History, S. & B. Webb, 1929.
   Life and Times of Sir Edwin Chadwick, S. E. Finer, 1952.

Index

THE PENNY

No 438.   FOR THE WEEK ENDING

THE ANDO

THE POOR PICKING THE BONES TO LIVE
See our Leader.

(From

WORKHOUSE ATROCITIES.—Just before the Prorogation of Parliament, Mr. Wakley a
in crushing bones, and that while so employed they were engaged in quarrelling with each ot
    With regard to the immediate case before us, it appears, from the investigation (obse
crushing bones collected from various sources, including frequently the bones of horses as well
    " They must have been ground down by hunger to a condition as low as that of the ve
bones,' and, ' as soon as one sees a good bone which is unobserved by the rest, he contrives t